D1664431

THE CULTURE CRE8OR

Table of Contents

Preface

In July 2016 I left the security of my principal position to venture out and pursue my passion of transforming culture in schools. For years I have been what I refer to now as a Culture Cre8or, someone who wants to create a community where everyone feels safe, valued, and appreciated. Even as a young girl, I wanted to provide everyone I met with a magical experience, whether it was family members who would visit our home or friends whom I played with at school.

When I became an educator and a school leader, I found myself prioritizing the culture of my classroom and school over everything else. One thing I learned early in my pursuit of creating a positive culture is that a positive life begins with you. I found that focusing on personal culture led to better relationships among students, teachers, and staff, and there was a willingness to go above and beyond an assigned job description to help create a place where teachers and students wanted to be, including me.

The culture of a family, organization, business, or any group for that matter is the combined energy of the people that make up that union, and the more team members can take responsibility for their outcomes, be aware of how they show up, and be open to people and ideas that may differ from their own, the more we can create healthy communities of peace. Setting goals, boundaries, and values (behaviors) creates communities where people feel psychologically and physically safe. This is what being a Culture Cre8or is all about.

In my first book, *The Beauty Underneath the Struggle: Creating Your B.U.S. Story*, I take readers on a journey of discovering themselves as they experience the tough times. Because it was written during the pandemic, when we were on lockdown, it was easy for people to identify the struggles we were facing—schools and businesses were closed, our loved ones were getting sick with the virus or losing their lives, and the political atmosphere was toxic, to say the least. We learned that our lives can be a potpourri of good times, celebrations, and struggles. These webs of experiences can be challenging for us, especially with all the changes we have experienced since COVID-19 turned our world upside down. I believe this moment has stressed the importance of caring for our mental and emotional well-being as we attempt to adjust to all the changes in our personal and professional lives.

This moment is about not only renewing our culture but renewing our minds to move beyond this moment, so that we can ultimately feel the freedom that comes from living in our peace.

Renewing the mind requires us to become more whole. It requires an understanding of how our thinking patterns and beliefs impact the way in which we experience life. This means that we should give attention to supporting and nourishing our mind so that it doesn't become weak, unable to deal with the complexities of today's world. Renewing our mind forces us to look within to determine our core beliefs and consider whether these beliefs about ourselves, others, or the world are serving us well or not. If there is one lesson we learned from COVID-19, it's that time waits for no one. Life is short, so we shouldn't waste time thinking too much about the past or worrying about the future. The time to live is now!

Many of us spend so much time searching for the answers to life's struggles when the answers we seek can be found within; we need only to ask the right questions. This is why I am excited to bring to you my second book, *The Culture Cre8or: A Principal's Journey to Shaping a School's Values, Goals & BEliefs.* My hope is that this book will become your personal guide as you create not only a positive work culture but a positive life. I believe that a positive mind creates positive energy, which will create positivity in schools and in our world.

Introduction

The word *culture* can mean many things to different people. It can describe a way of life, the arts, or the habits of a group of individuals. But for the purpose of our time together, culture is the attitudes, beliefs, expectations, and guiding values that an organization accepts. You cannot physically touch the culture of an organization; however, you can feel it the moment you walk into a building. It's the way in which members interact with one another and with their customers; it's their common language and their way of aligning to a shared vision and mission.

I first became intrigued by culture when I was a young girl. I grew up in a home where the culture was not very good. My parents had many disagreements, which fostered a culture of divisiveness among the children. Rarely were we courageous enough to engage in difficult conversations with one another, and when there was a conflict, it might end with people not speaking to one another for several days, weeks, or even years.

I remember getting on the bus in the morning to head off to school, and while most of the children were engaged in conversations with one another, many times I sat gazing out the window with no expression, always wondering what I could do to mend the relationships in my family. You see, I learned early that if you're around negativity, it impacts your ability to learn and be fully engaged in the present moment. I loved my family, and I wanted them to be happy, but unfortunately, I would also learn that happiness is an inside job—it was something you had to choose to BE.

As I grew older and became a teacher working with the Head Start organization, I realized that I had the opportunity to create my own culture with the students and families I served. In this preschool classroom, I tested my theory of creating a positive culture by setting expectations, finding ways to give students and families a voice in the process and modeling the behaviors I wanted to see. It was great!

With each new assignment—whether I was a teacher, curriculum coordinator, behavior specialist, or principal—I continued to practice and extend my learning in creating positive communities.

When I became the principal of an elementary school, we were recognized for having a culture that supported student leadership, and I was selected to accompany my superintendent to Southwest Airlines, where I would become further invested in understanding culture and how to create a safe, healthy environment, not just for students but for teachers as well. I began to seek opportunities to become a Culture Cre8or at the district level and was instrumental in starting a group known as the Game Changers along with other leaders in my district.

So it was no surprise to anyone when I decided to leave my job as a school principal in July 2016 to start my venture of helping schools create and sustain positive culture. I developed a program now known as Culture Cre8ion and have worked with hundreds of schools all over the country, teaching them not only how to create a positive community but how to sustain it.

Over the following pages, I will share what I've learned on this amazing journey to creating positive organizations and a positive life. My husband, Kermit, is a big part of my story and my #1 Culture Cre8or. Kermit has spent over twenty-five years in human resources, in the business sector as well as in education, coaching others on the importance of having a solid mission statement that will become the guide to everything they do in the organization. He often says, "You (the leader) are the guardian of the mission," which means that it is the leaders' responsibility to uphold the promises of the organization.

This book is my invitation to you to join us on this amazing journey to create not only a positive organization but a positive life. Now is your time to become a Culture Cre8or. Welcome to the journey!

1

Return to Grace

Matthew Mason quickly steered his midsize sedan through the busy traffic while dabbing at nonexistent sweat on his forehead. He was sure he was getting hot flashes from his bubbling anxiety, even though the air conditioner was blasting at full strength.

How on earth did he find himself back at Grace? he wondered for the umpteenth time, glaring intensely into his rearview mirror. Matthew rapidly tapped his fingers against the steering wheel, glancing at his watch, which had not been properly set for months. He had not been this nervous since the day he proposed to his wife. If anything, he should have felt pretty comfortable—after all, he was returning to the same district where he had gotten his start as an educator and an administrator. But this wasn't the case; his heart felt like it was going to leap out of his chest. Although he was familiar with the district and the school, Matthew couldn't shake his nerves as he thought about his return to Grace.

Grace Schools was a medium-sized suburban district consisting of ten elementary schools, four middle schools, and two high schools located in the city of Grace. Grace's superintendent, Adam Rodriguez, loved Grace Schools and often shared with others how the district held a special place in his heart. His father had served on the Grace school board long before he was hired to be the superintendent. After his father passed away, he had dreamed of leading the district that his father had loved so dearly, so this was a dream come true.

After the COVID-19 pandemic, three of the campus principals retired, and many teachers left the classroom to pursue other opportunities. Superintendent Rodriguez and his team had finally filled all their key leadership positions except for one: a principal position at Mercy Elementary School. This was going to be a huge challenge for the superintendent, finding someone not only capable of leading but willing to take on the most demanding school in their district.

Mercy Elementary had been designated the lowest-performing school for the past three years, and with the onset of COVID-19, many of its students had fallen further behind. Now the state was threatening to close the school if the overall student performance did not improve within the next three years. With one year left to show improvement, the new leader would have their hands full.

Mercy had not always had these challenges. In fact, Mercy was the first public school in the city more than fifty years ago. Mercy was the perfect partner to Grace and had been a staple in the community, not only because the school provided children with a great education but also because it was a great benefit to the community, as it connected parents with important resources to support their families. This is one of the reasons the community was dedicated to saving Mercy.

When Mercy first opened its doors, the district had decided to take Mercy's mission further by offering classes and resources for parents and caregivers to support them with their educational goals. The district provided workshops on résumé writing and career exploration and even parenting classes.

The school had gotten national attention and was featured on a couple of news shows that highlighted ways in which Mercy Elementary was helping the community. People from all over made donations to Mercy to retain the specialized staff that had been hired to support the unique needs of the families the school served.

The school ran well for several years, until enrollment decreased, and fewer families showed interest in the program. The decrease led to less donor support, so the program was eventually transitioned into a traditional public-school setting, leaving behind the neediest students and families in the community with staff that was poorly equipped to support their hardships. Mercy changed from a school motivated by compassion to one filled with animosity and hostility toward those it served, as many of the teachers and staff felt that being at Mercy was a punishment.

The outgoing principal finally made the decision to resign in lieu of termination, which opened the door for the district to hire a new leader. Now that Mercy was running out of time, the district needed someone who could clean up the mess that had been created over the past decade and transform the school out of its bottom-ranking status. Knowing only one person capable of accomplishing this near-impossible job, Superintendent Rodriguez turned to Matthew Mason.

Matthew was familiar with Mercy Elementary. He had been first hired there as a math teacher and taught for a short time before becoming an assistant principal at Grace Middle School. After teaching math for several years, he felt that becoming an administrator would allow him to make a greater impact. Each day he entered the school, he found himself so engaged in his work that he barely noticed when it was time to pack up and go home. Superintendent Rodriguez had not met many assistant principals—or even principals, for that matter—who were as dedicated, passionate, and full of energy as Matthew.

Matthew left Grace to work in a nearby district because he feared complacency and wanted a new experience. So when there was an opening for a principal position with a neighboring district, Matthew jumped at the opportunity without hesitation, and he landed the job.

Matthew was passionate about culture, people, and leadership. While many people viewed culture as something related to the workplace, Matthew believed that culture begins the moment we are born into our families. As a young boy, he would often find himself studying the dynamics of his own family, which he believed was the first organization he was exposed to and where he learned how to be a good leader.

His parents had a turbulent relationship and eventually divorced when he was fifteen, which resulted in the family being divided. As the oldest of six children, he always saw it as his job to mend the broken relationships. Becoming a teacher and a principal was no different. He wanted to create environments where people felt valued, connected, and safe. You would often find Matthew's head buried in some book on leadership, psychology, or self-improvement. He believed the culture was the most powerful influence in creating successful teams, families, businesses, and schools.

In college he was introduced to a leadership book titled *The Leadership Code: Five Rules to Lead By*, which solidified his philosophy of leadership. The authors revealed that "leaders must model what they want others to master. Leadership of others ultimately begins with the self. Individuals who govern themselves will be more able to lead others." From his earlier experiences in his own family and other organizations, he knew that the secret to becoming a successful leader was more about leading yourself and teaching others how to do the same.

Superintendent Rodriguez had witnessed firsthand Matthew's cultural style. As a teacher Matthew had a way of getting parents involved in the day-to-day process of the classroom. While other teachers complained about parent visitors, Matthew provided parents with classroom jobs, making them feel like a part of the community. Rodriguez recalled visiting Matthew's math class on occasion and watching parents work with groups of students, provide feedback on lessons, or work on other class projects—it was amazing to watch. As an assistant principal, Matthew created a Student Voice Program that provided students as young as kindergarten with an opportunity to share their thoughts and opinions about their education. No matter what role he had, Matthew was always finding ways to bring people together, and that's exactly what Mercy Elementary needed now. If there was one thing Matthew learned in his own family culture, it was that if there are signs of division among its members, darkness will enter.

Superintendent Rodriguez was confident Matthew would be the perfect leader for troubled Mercy. Convincing him to leave his current principal position wasn't going to be easy, but the fear of being rejected wasn't going to stop Rodriguez from approaching Matthew about the opportunity.

Even though he thought Matthew was obviously the right candidate for the job, his acceptance was still a gamble, given that he was still learning how to navigate parenthood with his wife. Taking on a project as challenging as rebuilding Mercy was going to be a highly taxing role for anyone, especially a new parent. The guilt of putting Matthew in such an unfavorable position at a poorly structured school weighed heavily on Superintendent Rodriguez.

Guided by his faith, he knew that his angels would ultimately lead him to find the perfect principal for Mercy. After much prayer, Superintendent Rodriguez set aside his worries and hit send on his email reaching out to Matthew about returning to Grace.

As if his prayers had been answered, Rodriguez received a response from Matthew a few days later regarding his interest in hearing more about the position. He was so overcome with joy after receiving the email, he jumped out of his seat and threw his hands in the air in celebration of his newfound hope for Mercy.

Over the next week, Superintendent Rodriguez and Matthew exchanged multiple emails and phone calls to discuss the expectations for the position. Because he would be taking over the school midyear, it would be a delicate dance to transition from a principal who had been there for several years. To Rodriguez's surprise, Matthew showed little sign of being discouraged by many of the problems that plagued

Mercy. As daunting as the task was to revive the school, Matthew was honored and wanted to help.

As with teaching, his time as a principal flew by so quickly that Matthew had almost forgotten it was work at all. Although he had only been in his new position for a short time, he loved it dearly and confidently felt that he was making an impact.

No one in his current district had any doubts about Matthew's abilities as a school leader; everyone expected he would one day excel to become a superintendent. His teachers and students hated to hear that he was leaving to return to Grace, but they knew that Mercy needed him much more than they did.

After wrapping up the interview process with Superintendent Rodriguez and his team, Matthew was named the new principal of Mercy at the next school board meeting. He immediately began preparing himself and his family for the transition. It would be a major change from working in a school with no major issues to leading one that was now on the verge of closing, but Matthew felt ready and up for the challenge. Although he felt confident in his abilities, he would quickly realize that his past experiences couldn't fully prepare him to become principal of a school whose academic infrastructure had fallen apart.

To best support her husband, Matthew's wife, Samantha, decided to leave her job in nursing to stay home with their six-month-old twin girls, Baelor and Bella. Samantha was Matthew's biggest cheerleader and was excited for him to take on this new role, as she believed in his ability to bring about change in any organization. Matthew attributed much of his success to his wife, whom he met in college and instantly fell in love with. For Samantha, all she wanted was for Matthew to be happy. He would often ask her how he could make her happy, and she always had the same response: "BE happy." Knowing he had the full support of his wife, to the extent that she was willing to put her career on hold, boosted Matthew's confidence that accepting the position at Mercy was the right decision, not only for him but for his family. However, the closer Matthew's first day in his new position approached, the more his confidence began to wane, and reality set in. Everything Matthew read about Mercy Elementary made him second-guess whether taking the job was right after all. Mercy was no longer a typical school environment. It felt like he was walking into an elementary war zone.

Matthew always felt he was put on this earth to use his talents to serve others, which was one of the many reasons he was a good leader. For him leadership was never a way to exercise his authority but rather to remind those he served that taking authority over their own lives would lead them to create the reality they had always wanted. This was what Matthew loved most about being a leader—reminding his teachers and staff of their power to create the life of their dreams—and that was what he did best.

Matthew ended the conversation he was having in his head as he pulled into the parking lot of Mercy Elementary. Superintendent Rodriguez was already standing there, waiting to greet him, his hands gripping two cups of coffee. Matthew exhaled deeply to calm his anxiety and dabbed his forehead once more with the handkerchief he had nestled in his fist.

There was no hiding from his first day now that the superintendent was staring him right in the face. He silently said the Lord's Prayer as he pulled into his designated parking space, taking advantage of the next few seconds before shifting the gear into park. He knew that once he exited the vehicle, he would truly be stepping into his role.

As soon as Matthew opened the car door, he was greeted by the voice of a nervous superintendent: "Only you can fix this, Matthew. The culture here is toxic, and the data reflects this. We can't think of a better turnaround person than you! Whatever is happening here, we know you will figure it out!" The superintendent extended a cup of coffee to Matthew.

Somehow the superintendent's anxious nerves brought some calm to Matthew as he took the cup of warm brew. It was just what he needed, since he had left home before he could make a cup. He transitioned the handshake into a solid hug, holding the superintendent in a tight grip for a few seconds and patting him a couple of times on his broad shoulders, careful not to spill his coffee.

"Well, good morning to you too," Matthew chuckled, slowly peeling away from the hug, hoping to make himself feel a bit more relaxed.

Matthew opened the back door of his car to retrieve his suit jacket and his backpack. He took the handkerchief he had been clutching during his drive and stuffed it into his pants pocket. He decided to keep it close, just in case his anxiety set in again.

There was no turning back now: he was officially the new principal of Mercy Elementary School. The men walked in unison up to the large double glass doors that outfitted the front of the school. As they pulled the doors open to reveal the small foyer, both men paused as if to say a silent prayer. Mercy's fate now rested in Matthew's hands.

2

Mercy, Mercy!

The interior of the school was far different from what Matthew remembered. The building used to smell of fresh, lemony floor cleaner and old textbooks, but now it was filled with the scent of rubbery sneakers, old whiteboard erasers, and ammonia from the boy's bathrooms. Matthew swallowed nervously as he proceeded forward beside his superintendent.

The hallways were empty, with a dim, subtle light that cautiously guided their path. They had decided it would be a good idea to meet at the school early to walk the campus before the rest of the staff arrived for the faculty meeting, where Matthew would be introduced as the new principal. With the winter holidays just ending, students had one last day of vacation before returning to a new year and a new semester. The faculty was scheduled to arrive later for their teacher workday.

As they strolled in silence, Matthew noticed an empty food wrapper lying on the floor of the hallway and faded bulletin-board paper with posters hanging by their last staple on the walls. It was a depressing scene. Matthew shook his head as the anticipation of what came next filled his heart with each step. The golden days of Mercy Elementary were truly gone, and there was no evidence of a real comeback.

Trying to find the positive was like being on a grueling scavenger hunt: it was a challenge. Matthew didn't want to spend his first day talking about the obvious; he really wanted to help the staff recognize the beauty underneath the struggle. However, everywhere he looked was only proof of the struggle.

"So, what do you think?" Superintendent Rodriguez asked with sincere curiosity, wanting to get Matthew's opinion about what he was experiencing.

"It's definitely not the Mercy I remember," Matthew replied hesitantly.

"Yes, a lot has happened since you left. But that's why I called on you, one of the best leaders I know, to turn back the clock and get Mercy back on track." The superintendent gave Matthew a couple of pats on the shoulder, trying to keep his confidence intact.

One good thing about the walk-through was having time to get reacquainted with the school he had once loved. Arriving at school before anyone else was always Matthew's favorite thing to do as a principal. It gave him time to appreciate the school without the distraction of students running around or teachers coming up to him with questions. This was his personal time to connect and reflect on the day ahead.

Although this was normally a time to take it easy and prepare for the day, the state of Mercy was such a shock to Matthew that he couldn't help but think about all the challenges he was up against. The further they ventured into the school, the more the school resembled an old dumping ground.

In addition to the litter on the floor, the school walls lacked any student achievements or even student work, a simple way to build morale and help students feel appreciated while motivating them to work hard. The beige walls in conjunction with the gray classroom doors made Mercy look more like an institution than a place for learning, especially for young children. Visually Mercy was nowhere near Matthew's standard of what a school should look like, especially one that would have students returning tomorrow.

And then there were the classrooms.

Given the state of Mercy's hallways, Matthew's expectations for the classrooms were not very high. As a math teacher at this same school, he knew how the classrooms used to look and what an engaging environment felt like.

Matthew believed that every area of the building should be used for teaching and learning. As a teacher he often ventured into the hallways, where he had encouraged his principal at the time to hang whiteboards so that teachers could expand learning beyond the walls of their own classrooms. It was an amazing experience to watch groups of students and staff doing lessons throughout the building. There was even a whiteboard outdoors in the courtyard. Now unused whiteboards that used to bring so much joy and excitement seemed to blend in with the walls, no longer having a purpose.

When Superintendent Rodriguez flipped the light switch in one of the first-grade classrooms, Matthew knew exactly why Mercy Elementary was in big trouble. The lights flashed on and illuminated wooden desks lined up in unorganized rows, most of them covered in faded marker scribbles that refused to come off. The walls of the classroom were just as empty as those in the hallways, as they also lacked evidence of classroom expectations, daily routines, or student progress.

While Matthew understood that many posters may have been removed prior to holiday break, he couldn't help but wonder if this was the normal state of classrooms throughout the school year. Matthew always felt that when even students and teachers weren't present in the classroom, the learning that took place should always speak loudly—from the arrangement of the desks to the work and bulletins that covered the walls. This was clearly not happening in this classroom; at least there was no evidence of it.

"How are any of the kids supposed to work and learn in such clutter?" Matthew asked aloud in disbelief.

"Like I said, this place needs a lot of work, and we want you to imagine what it could be. Can you do that?" the superintendent asked in his most encouraging voice.

Matthew knew how he wanted to respond, but somehow, he found a way to utter the "yes" that was buried deep in his subconscious and somehow managed to find a way to exit his lips. Matthew circled around the desks to look at the shelves of classroom supplies more carefully. Most of the marker sets were missing their caps, there were only a few pairs of scissors, and the trash cans were still filled with trash left over from before winter break. Entering each classroom was like déjà vu, repeating the same disorder and untidiness as the classroom before.

The last classroom they entered was the art room, and it seemed to be the brightest spot in the entire school. When they flipped on the lights, they were greeted by the most beautiful artwork. One wall displayed various renditions of the colors of the sun and moon, while the facing wall strutted abstract Christmas tree art in bright, vibrant colors. The room was well organized, its tubes of crayons, paints, and watercolors labeled and stored away neatly on their designated shelves. Although the tables wore a variety of faded paint and marker colors, it seemed to enhance the decor of the room, matching the vibrant energy that could be seen and felt throughout.

A classroom expectations poster was on display at the front of the room, and inspirational messages occupied vacant spaces. One poster read, "Sometimes You Have to Create Your Own Sunshine," while another read, "Mistakes are proof that YOU are TRYING!" For the first time since setting foot on campus, Matthew felt hopeful that something good was happening at Mercy.

"Do you remember this teacher?" Superintendent Rodriguez asked curiously.

"Is Ms. Helena still here?" Matthew asked in a slightly more upbeat voice.

"Yep! She's the best art teacher in the district, and despite the number of schools and districts that have tried to get her to leave, for some reason, she stays at Mercy," the superintendent said, scratching his head.

"Wow! Ms. Helena has been here for a long time! I loved working with her when I was here. She was always doing something for someone else." Matthew paused thoughtfully. "I'm so happy to hear she hung in there all these years. That says a lot about how special this school is," he said with a smile.

"We'd better get going so you can prepare to meet your new team," the superintendent suggested. "Plus, I want you to have time to enjoy your coffee."

Matthew had almost forgotten he was still holding his coffee in his hand. He was so engaged in the walk-through that he had not yet taken a sip.

As they prepared to leave the art room, Matthew paused, taking one last look and a deep breath in as he envisioned all the classrooms being filled with that same energy of creativity, inspiration, and hope. Just passing through Ms. Helena's classroom made Matthew feel a little more optimistic about the future of Mercy.

The final stop on Matthew's private tour was the principal's office. He nodded his head as he looked around the small space and exhaled. There were various forms and reports scattered all over the desk and a large pile that even spilled onto the floor. Folders were pulled out of place and messily stacked on a small conference-room table in the corner of the room.

"I know this isn't what you imagined, but I'm sure your administrative assistant, Ms. Rally, will help you pull everything together, Matthew," said Superintendent Rodriguez. "I have to jump on a quick call, so I'll see you in the library for the faculty meeting in an hour," he said, taking out his cell phone and backing out of the office. The superintendent gave a final wave as he exited the room and closed the door behind him, locking Matthew in his new little dungeon.

After walking the building, Matthew's optimism for the school year was now hanging by a thread. He had not completely lost hope, but to say it was going to take an endless amount of work was an understatement. Matthew sat down in the seat behind his office desk, set his backpack aside, and let his new responsibilities fully sink in—although he found it hard to concentrate with his predecessor's mug filled with old coffee still occupying the desk and a tornado of papers and folders in no particular order staring back at him. Using the outside of his hand, he slid the old coffee mug into the trash can beside the desk and replaced it with his fresh cup.

Matthew shook his head as he recounted the different places around the school. If he was going to help change the school's direction, he would need to address the culture—the attitudes, beliefs, and values of the school. From his brief walk this morning, the toxicity of the culture was loud and clear.

He recalled a book that his former superintendent had gifted him when he was hired as principal: *The Culture Code*, by Daniel Coyle. In the introduction Coyle shares his experience researching and visiting successful groups. He found that cultures are created by a specific set of skills that tap into the power of the social brain. He described the skills as follows:

Skill 1: Build Safety—explores how signals of connection generate bonds of belonging and identity

Skill 2: Share Vulnerability—explains how habits of mutual risk drive trusting cooperation

Skill 3: Establish Purpose—tells how narratives create shared goals and values

Coyle believed that these three skills work together to build strong connections that will lead to strong actions.

Matthew had relied on these three skills to drive his creation of a strong culture at his last school, but he questioned whether these skills would be enough to save Mercy. He had a hard time believing that anyone would be able to comfortably learn in such a disorganized and discouraging place, let alone children. However, Ms. Helena's art classroom was filled with inspiration and energy that every classroom could use. But how could he take what Ms. Helena had been creating for years and share it with the rest of the school? Could there be more teachers like Ms. Helena that may have simply lost hope? Would focusing on building safety, sharing vulnerability, and establishing purpose work in this case?

He placed his face in his hands, only to look up and find his coffee cup staring back at him. He removed the stopper that had been keeping the contents warm and took his first sip. It was the most delicious coffee he had had in a very long time. "A Cup of Peace," the label on the side of the cup read, and that's exactly how it made him feel, peaceful. He sat back and took a few deep breaths. Concentrating on the breath was his way of slowing the world down when everything seemed to be going a hundred miles a minute.

After placing the cup back on the desk, he noticed something written underneath the sleeve. "BE..." was displayed on the side with a bold, black marker. Matthew stared at the word for several seconds, wondering what the message could possibly mean. The word itself brought even more peace, and he almost forgot about his cluttered office space and the upcoming faculty meeting.

When he glanced at the clock on his laptop computer, however, he noticed that he had only a few more minutes before the staff meeting. He quickly took his notebook out of his backpack and began outlining his message to his new staff. Matthew never liked to rehearse what he was going to say—he always wanted to be authentic—so he often found himself simply creating bullet points of topics he wanted to go over. As he stared down at the blank notebook, his pencil seemed determined to do its part as he tapped it against the paper, waiting for the right message to come to mind.

Besides Ms. Helena's art classroom, his eyes had failed to iden-tify anything else that was good at Mercy, so he had to travel back into the heart of where it all started, the beautiful story of Mercy and its long history of service. This would help set the purpose as he shared Mercy's mission, values, and goals.

Before he knew it, he had drafted a page full of notes on everything that Mercy meant to the community. As he stared at his work, his heart became full of all the opportunities they had to revive this great school. He wrote down the three skills from the book his previous superintendent had given him: safety/connection, vulnerability, and purpose.

"You can do this. You got this! You go, boy!" Matthew repeated to himself as he stood up with his head held high and his hands on his hips. No matter how rough Mercy's condition was, he couldn't let that bring him down as its new principal. He knew that, as the leader, he had to help his team see the school with their hearts and not just with their eyes. Matthew once again stared at the word *BE…*on his coffee cup and then wrote it in bold letters at the very top of his notes as a reminder to be open and stay in the moment. "BE," Matthew said aloud before exiting his office.

3

BE...

Only five minutes separated Matthew from the long-awaited faculty meeting where he would come face-to-face with the people he would lead. Voices in the distance faintly filled the hallways as Matthew grabbed his notebook and what was left of his coffee and made his way to the library.

When he entered the meeting space, he noticed that many of the staff had not yet arrived, even though the meeting was scheduled thirty minutes later than usual to give the team a little extra time before coming into work. Matthew continued making mental notes, assessing the current culture of the school.

Superintendent Rodriguez stood at the door, greeting staff members with the newly appointed assistant principal, Ms. Reeves. Matthew had not yet met Ms. Reeves, but she had been at Mercy for almost three months, and this was her first job as an assistant principal.

"Good morning, Ms. Reeves, I'm Matthew," he said, extending his hand to greet her.

"So good to meet you. I've heard some amazing things about you, and I'm excited to work for you," Ms. Reeves said with a nervous smile.

"We'll be working together, Ms. Reeves—we're a team," Matthew said, returning the smile.

"Yes, that's what I meant, work *with* you, sir," Ms. Reeves responded.

Although Matthew hadn't had the pleasure of being a part of the assistant principal interviews for Mercy, he was happy that Ms. Reeves had been selected. After reviewing her work history, he learned that she had taught in an elementary school for several years in another state and had recently been promoted as an instructional specialist prior to moving to the city of Grace to follow her husband's job.

The superintendent had shared with Matthew that Ms. Reeves had glowing references and that the team was highly impressed with her interview. They thought she would be a bright spot for Matthew as the new assistant principal.

Although the teachers and staff were scheduled to be in their seats for the meeting by 8:30 a.m., so far only half had arrived and were ready to get started. Superintendent Rodriguez seemed unbothered, which made Matthew wonder how often this kind of tardiness happened.

By 8:35 a.m., most of the staff had taken their seats, which Superintendent Rodriguez took as a sign of "good enough" to start. Some of the teachers were on their phones, and others talked to their tablemates, while some yawned over coffee as the superintendent stood up to kick off the meeting.

Matthew could not believe the lack of respect the staff had for their superintendent. If this behavior didn't change, there was no way this team was going to get anything accomplished.

"Good morning, Mercy Elementary," the superintendent began. "I said, 'Good morning, Mercy Elementary,'" he repeated, after getting a halfhearted response the first time. "Today signifies a new day for this great school," he continued. A few giggles could be heard around the room when the superintendent referred to Mercy as "great."

"We have a well-respected former Mercy faculty member here to help us strive to be better and accomplish our new goals for Mercy. He was a math teacher at Mercy before becoming an assistant principal in our great district. He left Grace a few years ago and took his talents to a neighboring district, but now he's back! I'm very excited and proud to introduce Matthew Mason as the new principal of Mercy Elementary! Let's give him a warm welcome, please." Superintendent Rodriguez led a round of tepid applause.

Matthew straightened his tie as he stepped in front of the Mercy team. Some staff members showed interest in their new leader, sitting up straight in anticipation of his message, while others wore bored or disinterested looks and continued talking to their peers or looking down at their phones. A few others were still absent altogether.

Matthew brushed his hands across his blue slacks to wipe away his fears and positioned himself proudly in front of the room, ready to deliver his message. As he pulled out his notes, his eyes immediately gravitated to the word BE..., which he had written at the very top. A sense of calm filled his entire body as he flattened the paper on the rectangular table beside him.

"Thank you, Superintendent Rodriguez, for that kind introduction," Matthew said, staring directly into the eyes of his team as he scanned the room. "Who is Mercy?" he proceeded. The entire room came to a standstill, and one could have heard a pin drop on the worn gray carpet that covered the floors of the library.

Matthew allowed the question to linger in the air for a few moments before asking again, in a softer tone, as if he was saying it in a thinking voice, "Who is Mercy?"

The teachers and staff simply stared into Matthew's eyes or looked down at their tables, afraid to make a move in case any motion would indicate they wanted to respond. There was complete silence.

Suddenly a small voice broke through the stillness like a glass shattering. "Mercy is a school that stands for compassion and forgiveness. We used to be one of the greatest pillars in the community, providing support to those who needed it. That's Mercy!"

"Ms. Helena, thank you for that!" Matthew said, acknowledging the art teacher's contribution. "It's so good to see that you're still at Mercy. Can you share with the group why you've chosen to stay here all these years?" Matthew hoped Ms. Helena's comments could inspire a few people.

"I'm happy to see you too, Mr. Mason! Welcome to Mercy!" Ms. Helena said, rising to her feet. "I've been the art teacher here for twenty-one years. In my heart I know what Mercy has to offer students and families, and this is one of the reasons I stick around. Mercy's mission is all about helping the community. Our students and families used to feel safe here, and I have faith that we can bring that back. I love to serve, and what better place to do that than Mercy?" Ms. Helena said in her most sincere voice.

A few teachers rolled their eyes at Ms. Helena's comments, while others continued to talk or look down at their cell phones.

"Thank you, Ms. Helena," Matthew said, as he began strolling between tables and making eye contact with the staff. "Take a good look around this room. All of you have been selected to be at the best school in the district. It is no coincidence that you are here."

A few giggles erupted, as if Matthew had shared a good joke. "Mercy," Matthew went on, ignoring the laughs, "Mercy was built over fifty years ago. In fact, it was the first public school in the city of Grace. Because the city is called Grace, community leaders thought the name Mercy would send a message of compassion, kindness, and forgiveness for others. Mercy is the perfect companion to Grace and has been a staple in this community—not only because it provides children with a great education but also because it is a great benefit to our community, connecting parents with important resources to help them be successful. This is one reason the community has been so dedicated to saving Mercy. But you, my friends, and I have been carefully selected to lead this mission to save our beloved Mercy. So the question I have for you today is this: Are you ready?" Matthew looked around the room.

"You tell us—you're the leader!" a small voice replied from the back of the room. Despite the unprofessionalism, Matthew did not allow her comment to interrupt the flow of his message, especially now that more teachers were staring directly into his eyes and seemed to be showing interest in what he was saying.

"We are all leaders here at Mercy," Matthew continued, looking in the direction of the voice that had spoken out.

"You see, one leader cannot turn this school around. It's going to take all of us to lead," Matthew said. "And the greatest form of leadership is self-leadership. So, for the next few months, we will all learn more about ourselves as we prepare to save our dear Mercy."

The teacher from the back of the room spoke up again: "What do you mean, 'all of us lead'? You were the one hired as the principal."

"Thanks for your response. What's your name?" Matthew asked, curious to identify the person behind the voice that was already giving him a hard time.

"I'm Ms. Graves, and I've been teaching first grade for thirty years. Many of us didn't ask to be at this school; we were placed here," she shared.

"Nice to meet you, Ms. Graves," Matthew responded, forcing a smile.

"It's good to meet you, too, but can we speed things up? We've got a lot of work to do in our rooms before the students come back tomorrow, and I know everyone else in this room feels the same way. They're just afraid to speak up, so I speak for them," added Ms. Graves.

"I am aware of the time, Ms. Graves, and the expectation is that everyone can and will represent themselves. That's what I mean about self-leadership," he said calmly, looking around the room.

The room fell completely silent. Some staff members seemed shocked, while others were impressed that Matthew had the courage to push back against Ms. Graves on his first day.

Ms. Graves had been teaching first grade at Mercy for the last two years but had been transferred to several different campuses across Grace because she was known as a trouble-maker. Since Mercy was considered the dumping ground for poor educators, Ms. Graves ended up at Mercy. The district hoped she would retire soon and didn't know what else to do with her.

Turning his attention back to the group and away from Ms. Graves, Matthew continued walking at a slow, deliberate pace among the tables and resumed his conversation as if Ms. Graves had not said a word. If he had learned anything about teaching, it was never to give the desired attention to troublemakers; it would only give them more power to continue causing disruptions. In this situation, Ms. Graves was no different.

Ms. Graves became so upset that she was being ignored that she picked up her belongings and left the meeting. She stood in the doorway signaling for the folks at her table to join her, but only one person got up: Ms. Shields, who was known as Ms. Graves's trusty sidekick. She would often go along to get along with Ms. Graves because she didn't want to get on her bad side. The other teachers avoided eye contact with Ms. Graves, keeping their eyes glued to the front of the room as if they didn't know she was there.

"If we're all going to become leaders, we must first learn to lead ourselves," Matthew continued. "So, for the next few weeks, I'm going to challenge every person in this room to discover the leader within. This means thinking about your own gifts and how you can use these talents to move Mercy forward. This means examining your own personal values, ideas, and beliefs and assessing whether they are aligned to our mission here at Mercy. As you know, we have exactly one year to turn this school around, and I need to know that everyone in this room is up for the challenge. This will not be easy. We will need to push one another, encourage one another, and be honest with one another. Are you ready to turn Mercy around?" Matthew asked in his best football-coach voice.

Matthew could see a few heads nodding and heard a few barely audible yeses in the room.

"I will set up one-on-one meetings with each of you, en-suring that you can answer the call that Mercy needs right now," Matthew informed the group. "I will also be meeting with grade-level and department teams to map out our new strategy to turn this school around. If you're with me and you're ready to make Mercy one of the best places to work and learn in this district, let me hear you say, 'Yes! Yes! Yes!'" Matthew shouted the last three words with enthusiasm.

Matthew could hear a few more voices joining in. He grabbed his notes, which were still spread out on the table at the front of the room, to make sure he hadn't missed anything he wanted to say on his first day.

"BE," Matthew said to himself.

"There is one last thing I want us to do before we prepare for our students to return tomorrow.

"This morning Mr. Rodriguez greeted me with a cup of coffee, and although this is probably the best coffee I've had in a while, what I enjoyed even more was the message he wrote on the outside of the cup: "BE..." Matthew held the cup of coffee above his head for all to see.

"Think of the power in the word *BE*," Matthew suggested, still holding up his coffee cup.

"BE...to be mindful, to be alive, to be in this present moment with you," Matthew continued. "What does it mean to you?" Matthew paused again, giving the staff time to consider the question.

Matthew was very good with *wait time*, a term used by his mentor that refers to the deliberate pause after posing a question or the pause after a student's response. He found that many of the strategies he learned as a teacher worked just as well when working with adults. He realized that if he paused long enough, someone in the group would begin to feel uncomfortable with the silence and give a response.

"To BE aware!" said Ms. Helena with a smile.

"To BE aware," Matthew repeated. "Thanks, Ms. Helena! Anything else?"

"Tuning in to your body and mind!" another teacher responded.

"Yes! Tuning in to your body and mind!" Matthew repeated. "What's your name, and how do you contribute to this great school?"

"I'm Ms. Love, and I'm the counselor here," the woman said with a smile.

"Thank you for your contribution, Ms. Love," Matthew said, returning the smile.

"Before we can do anything, we first must BE," said Matthew, pausing to give his message a moment to sink in.

A teacher cautiously raised her hand from across the room. Matthew noticed her immediately and politely asked her name and how she contributed to this great school.

"Hi, Mr. Mason, my name is Ms. Thomas, and I teach second grade here," she said in a soft voice.

"Nice to meet you, Ms. Thomas. I love second grade! What is your question?" Matthew asked.

"This school has had a bad reputation, and many of us don't have many nice things to say because we're currently the lowest-performing school in the district, and we are reminded of that every day we step through those doors. Do you really believe we can turn this around? In a year?" Ms. Thomas asked in a sincere tone.

"That's a great question, Ms. Thomas. How many of you feel the same way?" Matthew asked, looking around at all the hands that were now raised toward the ceiling.

"Think about this. If you highlight all the bad things about your school, you are ultimately attracting more bad things," Matthew explained. "Researchers say that we have anywhere from 12,000 to 60,000 thoughts per day. At least 80 percent of these thoughts are negative, and 95 percent of them are the exact same thoughts we had the day before. Therefore, we must be more intentional, not only with our thoughts but also with our words. We get to choose who we want to BE, and that starts with how we think about our school."

Matthew knew that if they were going to transform the culture, he needed to change the way people thought about themselves and the school. One thing he believed about culture was that it is more of an inside job than it appears. So he knew he would have to get the team to reflect on their own values, behaviors, and beliefs if they were going to create a positive team culture.

"Every person in this room knows how they've felt about Mercy in the past. Today we're changing that! I want you to envision what Mercy can BE once we change our thoughts and the way we speak about our dear school. I want you to think of what it will take for you to make Mercy a great place to work and learn. Once you have that image, turn and share your vision for Mercy with your tablemates. What do you want Mercy to BE? I'll give you a couple of minutes to discuss!" Matthew said.

Teachers and staff immediately began sharing their thoughts and ideas with others at their tables. Matthew set the timer on his cell phone for two minutes and placed it on the table near the front of the room.

For the first time during the meeting, he turned and exchanged a smile with the superintendent. He had been so engaged with his new team that he had almost forgotten his boss was in the room.

The superintendent stood up, patted Matthew on the back, and informed him that he had another meeting to get to. He pulled Matthew's arm toward him and whispered in his ear, "I knew you were the one for the job. You've got this! Oh, and by the way, I had nothing to do with writing that word on your coffee cup. That message was from the universe." He gave Matthew a big smile before leaving the room.

Matthew smiled back at the superintendent. He had no solid plan for how he was going to turn this school around, and he knew that he would not be able to do it alone. This faculty meeting was only the BEginning.

4

A Purpose for BEing

Ding-dong, ding-dong. The timer went off on Matthew's cell phone, signaling that the two minutes were up. The conversations slowly came to an end as many faculty members' eyes focused back on Matthew.

"I'm excited to hear about your conversations. What is your vision for Mercy Elementary School? What would you like Mercy to BE?" Matthew asked again.

Many of the staff members sat quietly, looking around at one another. Others stared down at the table, hoping not to be noticed. Matthew stood motionless. After several seconds of waiting, a male teacher in the back of the room finally raised his hand.

"Hello, what's your name, and how do you contribute to this great school?" Matthew asked.

"Hello, I'm Joseph Simmons, and I'm the PE teacher," the man announced in a confident voice. Mr. Simmons was approximately five feet, four inches tall with a very muscular frame.

"Nice to meet you, Mr. Simmons! What is your vision for Mercy?" Matthew asked.

"Well, this is my first coaching position, and I like what you're saying. I didn't know that this school was the first public school in the city of Grace—I think that's cool. And I think we can bring Mercy back to what it was built for fifty years ago. I think you said it used to be a school of compassion, kindness, and forgiveness—I like that," Mr. Simmons declared.

"That's awesome, Mr. Simmons! We're bringing Mercy back!" Matthew said in his Justin Timberlake singing voice, for which he earned a few smiles and giggles.

"We want our students and teachers to be safe here," another teacher answered from the opposite side of the room. "Since COVID, we've lost the connection with others we so desperately need, and we want to feel safe again."

"Safety is definitely important! Our physical safety and our psychological safety," Matthew added.

"We will be the highest-performing school in the district!" another teacher exclaimed.

"Families will come from all over the state to enroll in our school because of the programs we provide!" a staff member added.

As more teachers continued to respond, Matthew grabbed a sheet of chart paper from the desk behind him and began jotting down their responses. The chart was a little over halfway full of hopes and dreams for Mercy when the engagement died down.

Matthew added the finishing touches to the chart by writing "BE" at the very top. The energy shift in the room was noticeable, and so were the few staff members who did not engage and sat with their arms crossed. Getting buy-in from the teachers and staff would be critical in turning the school around. Matthew knew that he wouldn't get all people on board with his plan, but he wanted to encourage as many people as possible to simply believe.

"All of your comments are great and exactly what we can achieve together when our energy is focused in the same direction," he said, pointing to the chart. "Making a great school does not happen overnight, nor does it happen with just one person. It may take weeks or even months, but with the collaborative efforts of all of us, I know we can do it! Together, we can save Mercy Elementary from closure!"

Matthew continued with an excited tone, "Look at all of the things you've shared about the Mercy we can create. Each and every one of us will need to care about Mercy just as we care for ourselves and our families. When we talk about Mercy, we must understand that we are in some way talking about who we are. Mercy is not only a place where we come to work; it is also our home—this is our family. We owe it to our students and ourselves to not only show up each day but show out!"

There were a few smiles and giggles after Matthew's comments. But more than anything, the people in the room could feel a sense of hope.

"Today is the first day that we take back our beautiful school and show ourselves what we are capable of when we can come together," Matthew said, walking toward the front right corner of the tables. He handed one teacher the chart he had used to write out their vision for Mercy. "Let's all sign this chart to solidify all that Mercy can BE!" he suggested.

The chart was passed around the room in snake formation, with a majority of the faculty members signing it with little to no hesitation. However, there was still a handful of teachers who were unmoved by the optimism that was now animating the room. Matthew noticed their furrowed brows and crossed arms from the corner of his eye but again refused to give negativity his attention. When the chart got to the last staff member in the room, the teacher stood up and handed it directly to Matthew without signing.

"Are you going to sign it?" Matthew asked the teacher.

"With all due respect, no. I wish I could believe in this romanticized idea you all have about next year, but it just seems a bit idealistic. Mercy's state isn't the result of just one or two years of neglect. It's been a long time in the making, and so it doesn't make sense that everything can improve in a fraction of the time," the man explained with shrugged shoulders.

"I understand your concern and appreciate your honesty. I never expected everyone to just blindly follow this vision for our dear Mercy. I want us to work together in a way that everyone's voice is heard. This chart," Matthew said, holding it high for everyone to see, "is a lot, but it is certainly not impossible. Don't allow yourself to be limited by your doubts." He paused as he secured the chart on the wall behind him before signing it himself.

"I had an opportunity to walk the building this morning and noticed that most of our classrooms and hallways are simply not ready for students tomorrow. Let's do a thorough sweep for trash and missing supplies as we prepare for learning. I would like each team leader to provide me with a report on your team's needs. If we're going to create a positive vision," Matthew said, pointing at the chart, "then we must first clear the mud from our windshields, don't you think?

"Before we leave, I want to invite everyone to join me in a positive energy circle," Matthew said.

"I love starting meetings on a positive note and ending with something positive. A positive energy circle is a time for us to come together and share something that inspires us—it could be a quote, a poem, or even a thought. I would like for you to try this with your students," Matthew said as the staff members stood up to join him in the circle.

"Remember, the way you start and end each day is very important, and I like to start and finish with an inspirational thought or idea," Matthew shared.

"For our positive energy circle today, let's think of *one word* that's going to inspire you as you work in your classrooms today," he instructed.

Hopeful, stressed, grateful, curious, blessed, anxious, encouraged, positive, BE—these were just a few of the words that rang out within the circle. Each word uttered by a staff member seemed to bring encouragement to the entire team. It was a successful first meeting.

"Thank you, everyone! Let's bring Mercy back!" Matthew stepped out of the circle and ended the meeting.

The library cleared out as teachers and staff returned to their respective spaces. Several teachers came up to thank Matthew personally for being there, and some wanted him to know that they enjoyed his message and felt renewed.

Ms. Helena, the art teacher, came up and gave Matthew a big hug. "It's so good to see you," she said with a smile. "You know, Ms. Rally, the secretary, and I are the only ones left from the original crew."

"Good to see you're still here! Your classroom looks just as amazing as it did when I was a teacher here. It really gave me hope for Mercy," Matthew said with a warm smile.

"Yes! Yes! Yes!" Ms. Helena said before gathering her things and leaving the library.

Although Matthew knew his office needed to be cleaned just as much as the classrooms, he decided he could stay late and clean his office after all the teachers had left the building. He was more interested in the rest of the staff and thought this would be a good time to walk the building and establish connections.

Matthew walked to each classroom and spoke with teachers, aides, and custodial staff. He even checked in on the cafeteria team. Teachers and aides were busy clearing out clutter and organizing their classrooms, the custodial staff was running through cleaning supply inventory, and the cafeteria staff was sanitizing the kitchen to ensure health standards were being met. Overall, the staff seemed enthusiastic.

Posters, routines, and organization charts were necessary but would require more time and effort than teachers could offer in just one day. Everyone had a lot of work to do to prepare the building for learning.

After all the staff had gone home for the day, Matthew stayed an extra three hours organizing and rearranging his office. Once his office was set up, he finally had time to boot up his computer and check emails for the day. When he opened his inbox, there were so many new messages, it was like he had missed out on an entire month of communication.

Matthew responded to a few messages that required his immediate attention, then opened a blank Word document and began to take notes on everything he had noticed on his first day, including the progress being made and additional steps that were still necessary. Matthew was very reflective and often thought about how he responded to various situations and how his actions and decisions impacted others.

The faculty meeting had been a good start toward the team's new vision for Mercy. However, a positive vision and tidying up was only the tip of the iceberg for rescuing this school on the verge of closure. Matthew leaned back in his seat and inhaled slowly, staring at the BE chart the team had created. He had no clue how they were going to make half of those things happen in such a short time, but he knew his role as a leader was to support the staff in believing that all these things were possible.

Matthew knew that he had to make the most efficient decisions in the shortest amount of time now that school was starting tomorrow. He also knew that he couldn't let any distractions get in the way of progress, which meant addressing unwanted behaviors from the start.

He took out the notebook that he had used to record those team members he needed to address from today's meeting. He opened a fresh email and started a new message:

"Dear Ms. Graves…"

5

The Best Journey
Takes You Home

Matthew wanted to schedule time to speak with Ms. Graves about abruptly leaving the faculty meeting, but he also realized that she was a big influencer on campus, so he wanted to be careful in the way he approached her. He knew that she could make his life a living hell, but he also knew that if he didn't address her attitude, he would be allowing this behavior to become a part of the new culture he was trying to inspire. Culture was going to happen whether he liked it or not, but Matthew was determined to be intentional about the culture he and the rest of the staff created.

After contemplating what to write, Matthew wiggled his mouse to wake up his sleeping computer and drafted the following message:

Dear Ms. Graves,

Thank you for introducing yourself during the staff meeting yesterday. I would enjoy getting to know you better as we work to move Mercy forward. I would like to schedule some time to talk about your concerns during the staff meeting. We will send someone to cover your class this morning. Let's plan to meet in my office at 9:30, after the morning assembly.

I look forward to seeing you.
Mr. Mason
Principal
Mercy Elementary

"Education is not preparation for life; education is life itself." —John Dewey

#ReviveMercy #CultureCre8or

Matthew saved the email and scheduled it to go out at 7:30 a.m. the following morning. He did not want to take a chance on Ms. Graves checking her email that evening and worrying all night about the meeting. He remembered how anxious he would get when his principal sent out late-night emails; just the thought of an unexpected meeting or discussion made him so nervous that he often had difficulty sleeping. He finally learned to stop checking work emails at night and simply wait until the next morning to catch up. He made a vow to himself that he would not send late emails unless it was completely necessary.

Matthew powered down his desktop, put on his suit jacket, and grabbed his backpack. Before leaving his office, he paused for a moment and thought about all he had accomplished on his first day: he had had a good meeting with staff, which resulted in the team coming up with a positive vision for Mercy; he had an opportunity to visit with teachers and staff as they prepared for students' return; and his office was slowly coming together—all it needed was a few family photos, some motivational posters, and maybe a small plant.

He took one last look at the BE poster adorned with staff signatures that was currently the only piece of decor accessorizing the plain white walls of his office. Matthew shook his head in disbelief, unsure of how all those dreams were going to happen, especially in such a short period of time. He turned out the lights. As he walked down the long, dimly lit hallway, he realized that the building would be filled with students the next morning. He was excited to meet them, as they would be a reminder of *why* he had returned to Grace in the first place—to bring a sense of peace back to this community.

Approaching his car, Matthew heaved a sigh of relief as he noticed the vacant parking lot. He threw his backpack on the passenger-side seat and set his sights on the journey home to see his family. Home always provided him with a sense of serenity, and he couldn't wait to catch Samantha up on all that had happened on his first day.

On his drive home, Matthew thought about his upcoming meeting with Ms. Graves and how she might react to their discussion. He didn't have a set agenda for the meeting, but he knew that if he was going to change the culture at Mercy, he needed to set boundaries for the staff so that they could focus on the students. Matthew planned to have a one-on-one with each employee on campus, no matter their role. His goal was to accomplish this within the first two weeks of school so that he could get to know each team member and how they could contribute to saving Mercy. He still had not had an opportunity to meet with his secretary, Ms. Rally, or his new assistant principal, Ms. Reeves, so he still had a lot to accomplish.

When he finally arrived home, he found Samantha asleep on the living room sofa with Baelor and Bella resting beside her in their bassinets. His wife had made his favorite meal, spaghetti with Italian sausage, and even prepared a special plate just for him that was covered in plastic wrap. There was a note beside the plate that read, "I hope you had a wonderful day! Heat this up and enJOY!" Samantha always had a way of making him feel loved. He removed the wrap, placed the dish in the microwave, and walked over to plant a soft kiss on Samantha's forehead.

Matthew picked up Baelor, who was already awake, and held her close to his heart. He missed moments like this and wanted to make sure he didn't get so lost in saving Mercy that he lost what was most important—quality time with his family.

After spending a little time with the girls, he ate his dinner and retreated to the bedroom, leaving Samantha and the babies in their favorite resting space in the living room. His update would have to wait until morning, since he knew that Samantha needed her rest just as much as he did. Tomorrow was going to be another long day for him, so he wanted to make sure he got plenty of rest.

6

A Cup of Peace

Matthew tossed and turned the entire night thinking about all the things he needed to do. The mock conversation with Ms. Graves played out over and over in his mind like a broken record. She could easily become one of his biggest challenges, and he knew the results of today's meeting could determine how she would respond to his leadership from this point forward.

"Ready for your big day, big guy?" Samantha asked as she entered the bedroom with Baelor and Bella cradled in each arm. Although these were their first children, Samantha was already a pro at taking care of them. Matthew was always amazed at how good she was with the girls.

Matthew sat straight up in bed as Samantha placed one of the babies with a bottle in his arms. She proceeded to brush her teeth while Matthew stared down at Bella, looking into her beautiful brown eyes. She seemed to have grown a little overnight.

"How did you sleep, honey?" Matthew asked his wife, never taking his eyes off his baby girl.

"I think we had an okay night," Samantha responded. "They seem to tag team me in the night, making sure I don't sleep too long," she chuckled.

"So…how was yesterday? Sorry I was asleep when you got in last night, but I was excited to hear details about your first day," Samantha continued.

"It was good, definitely better than I expected," Matthew said. "My staff meeting went well, and the team came up with a positive vision for Mercy." Matthew finally took his eyes off his daughter to appreciate his wife's beautiful face.

Matthew thought Samantha was the most gorgeous woman he had ever seen. They first met in college and had taken a course together in which they were placed on the same team to complete a project. Matthew was so taken away by her beauty that he could barely concentrate on the project at all. He eventually got up enough nerve to ask her out on a date, and the rest became history. They were married shortly after.

Samantha quickly wiped her face and joined Matthew in bed, who was now holding Baelor.

"I'm not surprised you had an awesome day. I knew you would be great for this community," Samantha said, smiling up at her husband.

They shared a quick kiss, and then Matthew carefully returned Baelor to Samantha, got up, and proceeded to the bathroom to turn on the shower. He liked his shower extra hot, so he turned on the water a few minutes in advance before jumping in to make sure it was nice and toasty.

As he waited for the water to heat up, he stood in the doorway of the bathroom and stared into the mirror. *BE.* There was something about that word that still rang out in his mind, and it was enough to calm him down, despite his distress about Mercy. "Tuning in to the mind and body," he said to himself, repeating what Ms. Love, the counselor, had said *BE* meant to her. It was just the message he needed yesterday, and the coffee wasn't bad either.

His mind was running a mile a minute, but being with his family helped momentarily slow everything down. After enjoying a moment of peaceful mediation, Matthew greeted his hot shower.

Refreshed and ready to start the new day, Matthew got dressed, styled his hair, and gave himself one final look in the large bathroom mirror.

"Look at my big man! Handsome as ever," Samantha said, giving him a flirty grin.

"Thank you, honey," Matthew said, kissing Samantha and both of his girls on the forehead.

"Are you ready for another great day?" Samantha asked, holding the back of his head and pressing his kiss a little deeper into her forehead.

"As ready as I'll ever be," he admitted with a heavy sigh. "I have to address one of the teachers who left during the meeting yesterday. She could easily be my biggest problem this year."

"Yes, better to address those things now rather than wait. You are an amazing leader, and I know you'll do what's right for Mercy. You can't carry all the weight yourself. Rely on those who are willing to help. I love you, Matthew, and I believe in you," Samantha said with a warm smile. She loved supporting her husband and would often give him mini pep talks when he was faced with challenging situations.

"Thank you, honey. I really needed to hear that this morning," Matthew said before grabbing his backpack and heading toward the door.

"I would make you coffee, but the machine is broken again. I ordered the part, but it's going to be several weeks before it arrives due to the supply-chain shortage," Samantha said before Matthew could exit the room. Each morning Matthew and Samantha usually shared a cup of coffee. It was their way of making sure they spent time together before the day got away from them.

"Don't worry about it. I can grab a cup on the way into work," Matthew shared on his way out.

"Love you," Samantha called out.

"Love you more!" Matthew shouted.

The sky was still dark and full of clouds when Matthew reached his car. There was no forecast of rain, yet without the sun, the sky looked like it was about to burst into a full-blown storm. It felt like an ominous sign for the first day of school with students in the building.

Matthew pulled out of the driveway and tried his best to focus on all the things that had gone well on his first day. If he had learned one thing in his thirty years of being on this earth, it was that whatever you choose to focus on will expand, so he was constantly seeking the good. He tried his best to visualize a good outcome from the meeting with Ms. Graves, but for some reason his mind refused to believe the positive picture he was trying to paint.

"The hallways are going to be filled with a new class of kids, completely unique and different from the last time I worked at Mercy. It'll be nice to work with children and families again. I get to help revive one of the best schools in our community," Matthew nodded, staring into the rearview mirror. In addition to Samantha's pep talks, he often gave himself positive talks prior to heading into work. Matthew had learned to become his own personal coach.

After a few minutes of driving, he noticed the clock on his dashboard read 5:25 a.m., which meant he was going to arrive at Mercy much earlier than he had planned. Matthew still had time to stop for coffee, so he decided to look for coffee spots close to campus. So much had changed since the last time he and Samantha lived in Grace, and it seemed that new businesses were popping up everywhere.

As he drove through the familiar streets, he noticed a coffee shop he'd never seen before called A Cup of Peace. Matthew remembered the name from the coffee cup the superintendent had handed him the day before. He was immediately intrigued and followed his instinct to pay a visit himself. The name itself was so inviting that it acted like a gravitational pull, drawing him in. Peace was just what he needed before he started his day.

As Matthew pulled into the empty drive-thru lane and stared at the menu, he heard the most relaxing music his ears had ever encountered. It took him a few seconds to notice that the instrumental music was coming from an in-ground speaker.

As his attention drifted back to the menu board, his eyes were greeted with inspirational names like Angelic Americano, Mindful Mocha, and Love a Latte. The music, fused with the moving names of the coffee offerings, was already putting his mind and body at ease.

"Good morning! We're so happy you're here. Whom do I have the honor of serving this morning?" a voice chimed in softly, interrupting the intimate moment he was having with the music and menu board.

"Good morning! I'm Matthew," he said, scanning the menu to make his selection.

"Good morning, Matthew! I'm Cindy. What can I get started for you this beautiful morning?" the woman asked.

"I'd like a large Angelic Americano—black, please," Matthew decided after a minute of contemplation.

"Great! One large black Angelic Americano it is! We look forward to seeing you at the window," Cindy responded, ending the conversation with just as much enthusiasm as when she started.

Matthew couldn't wait to meet the face that belonged to the cheerful voice. How could she be so jovial so early in the morning? he asked himself. When he arrived at the window, an older woman with a huge smile on her face greeted him once more. How he wished he would see this same smile on many of the teachers' faces later this morning.

As he peered into the drive-thru window to get a glimpse of the rest of the team, he noticed that every person inside had the same cheery look on their face as the group worked together seamlessly. One person was in charge of the register, while another managed the coffee machine. This person signaled to the next team member to fill each cup to the brim before handing it to Cindy, who then placed a sleeve on it before passing it out the window. He watched in complete awe at their smooth operation.

"Hi, Matthew, pleasure meeting you!" Cindy beamed brightly as she exchanged Matthew's coffee for his credit card. He reciprocated her enthusiasm by smiling back.

"Fantastic!" Cindy exclaimed as she retrieved the credit card. "How are you this morning, Matthew?"

"To tell you the truth, this is my first full day at my new school, so I'm a bit nervous. So I could use 'a cup of peace' this morning," Matthew admitted with an embarrassed chuckle.

"Are you the new principal at Mercy Elementary?" Cindy asked with a curious look on her face.

"Yes, I am," Matthew responded, surprised that she knew.

"Superintendent Rodriguez comes by every morning, and he has been bragging about what a wonderful leader you are," Cindy said. "We are all rooting for you to save our dear Mercy." She smiled softly.

"Thank you so much; that means a lot," he responded. Matthew counted this as one of the good things that would hopefully expand during his day.

"The coffee is on us this morning! Remember, 'the moment you take responsibility for everything in your life is the moment you can change anything in your life,'" Cindy said, returning Matthew's credit card.

"Yes! That's Hal Elrod!" Matthew said, surprised. Cindy had referenced one of his favorite authors. He had read *The Miracle Morning* three times, which had encouraged him and Samantha to spend time meditating, exercising, and journaling before heading off to work.

Matthew pulled away dreamily as Cindy's words echoed in his mind. "The moment you take responsibility for everything in your life is the moment you can change anything in your life," he repeated to himself. In order to get the results he wanted, he couldn't waste any time thinking about who was responsible for Mercy's downfall; he would have to take 100 percent responsibility for the state of Mercy. He slowly sipped his Angelic Americano, trying to savor the taste as well as the experience he had at A Cup of Peace.

7

Mercy Eagles

Matthew's state of tranquility came to a sudden halt as he pulled into the parking lot of the school. He took a moment to take several deep breaths before going inside. In less than two hours, students would occupy the building, and the clock determining Mercy's fate would begin ticking. With every breath he took, he tried to imagine breathing in the good air that would give him energy to get through his day, while letting go of any doubts that tried to take over his mind. He said a quick prayer, grabbed his coffee, and exited the car—the new semester had officially started.

The hallways of the school were cold and quiet, as expected, when Matthew walked through the doors. He went straight into his office to prepare for the morning assembly with students and his meeting with Ms. Graves. He was relieved to see a mostly tidied building, especially after the hurricane state it was in yesterday.

Matthew set his backpack down behind his desk and stopped in front of the wall of filing cabinets to look for Ms. Graves's employee folder. He wanted to learn more about her, which he hoped would help with his discussion.

Matthew pulled her file and tucked himself into the large office chair behind his desk. As he flipped through her folder, he could see that Ms. Graves had been to several other schools in the district and had multiple corrective-action memos in her file. Matthew's eyes grew wider with each document he read. She had been reprimanded for things like yelling at a student, being late for work, staging a walkout with teachers, and leaving students unattended in the classroom. Ms. Graves was not only a troublemaker but a safety issue. How did she manage to stay in the system for thirty years? Matthew wondered.

Matthew closed his eyes and rubbed the palm of his hand on his forehead. At the end of her file was a growth plan dated the previous school year; however, the last principal had not followed through with documenting any of the action items they had agreed to.

The worrisome thoughts that had occupied his mind all night sprinted back into his head all at once. From outside his window, he could hear the faint chatter of teachers arriving now that school hours were close to starting. He quickly returned Ms. Graves's file to the cabinet and ran through his inbox to check for any emails that required his immediate attention before the student assembly. He took another sip of his Angelic Americano, which instantly reminded him of his visit to the coffee shop. Thankfully even the memory of the experience gave him a sense of peace.

After he was done checking emails, Matthew wanted to make sure he was present to greet the teachers and students as they arrived. He put on his suit jacket and jetted out the door.

As principal, he wanted to set a positive example by modeling the behaviors he wanted to see in the building. If he wanted teachers to greet students, he would need to greet teachers. He made sure he smiled as he walked by each teacher's classroom, bidding them good morning and asking if they had everything they needed to begin their day.

He could tell that the teachers were not accustomed to this from their principal. Many of them looked at him in shock, while others shook their heads, never making eye contact, and continued what they were doing. He tried not to take their behavior personally, but it was hard, especially since he was trying to show support and build connections.

As he walked the hallways, he enjoyed seeing the students laughing and talking to one another. What he didn't like was how staff members who were on morning duty sat in chairs yelling at students and shouting directions. "Don't eat that in the hallway!" "Pull your pants up!" "Stop running!" He couldn't believe how angry the staff seemed so early in the morning.

He knew this wasn't a great way for students, or staff for that matter, to begin the school day.

He also noticed many of the teachers and staff engaged in their own personal conversations rather than greeting students as they entered the building. Matthew quickly walked by, greeted the staff on duty, and politely asked them to stand up and greet students with a positive tone. There was so much work to be done, and correcting poor habits was now at the top of his list; he didn't have time to schedule a meeting for every negative behavior, so he decided this was important enough to correct on the spot. While the staff complied with his directives, he could tell that they were not pleased with his requests by the way they looked at him with intense eye contact and a clenched jaw.

Matthew had little time to worry about the morning procedures right now. He was only a few minutes away from starting the assembly with students, where he would introduce himself as their new principal.

Matthew had suggested having an assembly so that he could take the time to introduce himself to students, just as he had with the teachers. However, many staff members opposed the assembly. They said that students didn't know how to behave during these gatherings, which is why they had suspended doing them altogether. Matthew knew that students' poor behavior was not a good reason to eliminate assemblies; they needed to work with students and set proper expectations.

By 8:30 a.m. most of the students had arrived in the gymnasium for the morning assembly. Matthew felt pretty pumped up about meeting the students for the first time and building relationships with them. It was strange walking the halls as students arrived and having none of them know who he was. This was one of the perks of being a teacher and a principal: having the students treat you like a rock star. As he reached the double doors to the gymnasium, he was immediately greeted with a crowd of rowdy students sitting on the floor as some teachers leaned against the walls, unengaged. Matthew walked in, cleared his throat, and grabbed the microphone off the stand at the front of the gym.

"When I say 'Mercy,' you say 'Eagles,'" Matthew chanted into the microphone several times, trying to gain the students' attention. He then stood quietly for a few seconds, scanning the room and waiting for the students to settle down. However, they showed little interest in who he was or what he had to say.

"Good morning, Mercy Eagles," he called out in a clear and loud voice. Matthew paused again, waiting for all eyes to fall on him as the room slowly settled down. "My name is Mr. Mason, and I am your new principal." Most of the students looked up at him blankly, not fully understanding the significance of his arrival.

Matthew noticed that most of the students' behaviors resembled those of the teachers. There were groups of students who continued to talk while he was speaking, in the same fashion as the teachers who engaged in their own conversations.

"For many years I walked through these hallways and spent most of my day in the same classrooms as you do. Granted, I was a teacher and not a student, but I was here to learn and grow to be better than I was the day before, just like you. And that's what I hope to achieve here as your new principal." Matthew's eyes swept across the students and teachers as he walked slowly into the crowd.

To his surprise, several students cheered with great enthusiasm at his announcement. Matthew didn't know if the cheers were just an opportunity to make noise or if the kids were genuinely happy that he was their new principal. Either way, it made him feel proud. The roar of energy was a great way to boost his morale on his first day. Even though the assembly was short, Matthew wanted to end things on a high note to leave a positive and lasting impression on kids. He ended the assembly the same way he began: "When I say 'Mercy,' you say 'Eagles'! Mercy!" he said in a loud voice. "Eagles!" the students chanted back.

8

BE Responsible

The assembly ended, and the teachers gathered their students and headed back to their classrooms, with the exception of Ms. Graves. Her students looked around at each other, confused, as they followed the teacher's assistant who had been asked to take over her class so that she could meet with Matthew.

Ms. Graves stood with her arms crossed and a bored look on her face as she waited by Matthew's office door for their meeting. Matthew felt like a teacher again, watching a rebellious student who was sent to the principal's office.

"Good morning, Ms. Graves, I'll be with you in just a minute," Matthew said, trying to hurry in and prepare for the meeting. He grabbed his coffee, which was still waiting on the desk, and moved it with his notepad to the small conference table. He noticed that the word *BE* was handwritten on the cup again, but this time more text followed, "*BE Responsible* 100 percent," he read after moving the sleeve to uncover the message. Suddenly he remembered his conversation with Cindy from the coffee shop. She had mentioned a quote from Hal Elrod: "The moment you take responsibility for everything in your life is the moment you can change anything in your life."

Like yesterday, this message seemed to arrive right on time, just before he began his meeting with Ms. Graves. He knew that he had to take 100 percent responsibility for the state of Mercy, even if he wasn't responsible for hiring the team or for the low scores. If he was going to move the school forward, he couldn't blame the last principal, the teachers, the families, or the district. He would need to own everything, including Ms. Graves.

Matthew opened the door and invited Ms. Graves inside to have a seat. He sat across from her and started with "good morning" and small talk to keep things light before diving into what he needed to discuss.

"I wanted to talk to you about the staff meeting yesterday, Ms. Graves," Matthew started, after his unsuccessful attempt to engage her in pleasantries.

"What's there to talk about?" she asked in a sarcastic tone, taking out a notebook and pen from her bag and opening to a blank page.

"Well, you stated that you were the voice for the group, and you also walked out of a mandatory meeting before it was over. So I wanted to give you an opportunity to explain," Matthew continued. He kept his hands placed neatly on the table, open to hearing and understanding Ms. Graves's point of view. He wanted to make sure Ms. Graves felt as comfortable as possible.

"I told you we had something to do, but you wouldn't listen. So I took it upon myself to do what I thought was right," Ms. Graves pushed back arrogantly, staring directly at Matthew.

Matthew couldn't believe the disrespect that Ms. Graves had on display, especially since he was trying his best to communicate and understand her needs. He took a mental breather as he tried to maintain his composure. No matter what she said or did, he planned to remain professional and not give in to her disrespectful behavior. He glanced at his cup. "BE Responsible 100 Percent" was staring him right in the face. He took a deep breath in and exhaled slowly before continuing the conversation.

"Ms. Graves, if we're going to achieve this," Matthew said, pointing at the BE poster the team had created the day before, "then we need to work together, don't you agree?"

Ms. Graves glanced at the poster and slowly shook her head. "Do you really believe you can do all that?" she asked, answering her own question with a giggle.

Matthew's patience was being stretched to new limits as he restrained himself to maintain a calm demeanor. Ms. Graves's condescending remarks were beginning to get to him, but again he reminded himself that he was modeling the behavior he expected to see in everyone. BE..., he thought to himself again, staring at the poster.

"I don't think it's possible to transform the school alone," Matthew admitted. "But I do believe it can be accomplished if we all work together."

"I'm not sure any of us want to work with you," Ms. Graves said matter-of-factly, still looking at Matthew.

"You don't get to decide what others want, Ms. Graves. You will need to be responsible for your behavior and your behavior alone," Matthew said, taking the words directly from his cup. "And if you're saying your choice is not to work with me, then we have a bigger problem." Matthew was trying to set boundaries for her disrespectful tone. He still couldn't believe that he had to treat an adult on his team the same way he might lecture a small child.

"Is that a threat?" Ms. Graves questioned, raising her pen and positioning it to take notes.

"It's not a threat, Ms. Graves. However, the circumstance is real. For us to move Mercy forward, we can't have these types of distractions. Therefore, I am asking that if you have a problem with something I've said or done, you come to me privately instead of announcing it in the presence of the entire group. Secondly, you will need to get permission to leave a meeting early. It's not okay that everyone is asked to attend meetings, but some are allowed to leave unannounced. Understood?" Matthew asked with a stern tone.

"Sure." Ms. Graves shrugged nonchalantly as she closed her notebook. "I hope you address the other person who left and you're not just picking on me." The audacity for her to mention Ms. Shields when she was the one who prompted her to leave, Matthew thought to himself. Still, Matthew knew he had to address Ms. Shields, who left the meeting when Ms. Graves signaled her to follow.

"This meeting is strictly about you and your behavior, Ms. Graves. Do you have any questions about these expectations moving forward?" Matthew asked.

"No, not at this time," Ms. Graves responded, never looking up from her notebook.

"Thank you for coming in. I will follow up with an email regarding our discussion." Matthew ended the meeting with a forced smile.

They both stood up. Matthew escorted Ms. Graves to the door and wished her a good day, closing himself alone in his office. Matthew knew that the conversation had not gone well, but he felt good that he had taken responsibility and addressed the situation. He knew that this was probably not the last time he would meet with Ms. Graves. He also knew that he would need to follow through on correcting other unacceptable behaviors. If he didn't do something about her quickly, she could take up a great deal of his time.

He grabbed his cup of coffee, which had now cooled, to momentarily give himself something else to focus on. Being responsible was something the staff needed to work toward as he thought of ways to reinforce this message throughout the school. Matthew stared at the message again and allowed himself to dream of a school where students and staff took 100 percent responsibility for their thoughts, actions, and results.

Matthew realized that one of the biggest problems facing the culture at Mercy was the team's inability to take ownership of what was happening in the school. It seemed that everyone wanted to place the blame somewhere else, which didn't give them the power to solve the problems. If they were going to make anything on that BE poster a reality, they would first need to own all the things that were going wrong.

Matthew pulled out a book from his box of belongings that he had brought to work. He had been introduced to the book years ago, when he and Samantha first got married. Matthew was at a very low point in his life, and he blamed his parents and his upbringing for everything that was not going well.

Samantha, who had read the book with a friend, approached Matthew and asked him to read the first page. After reading the first page, Matthew was so inspired that he ended up reading the entire book. The book was titled *The Success Principles: How to Get from Where You Are to Where You Want to Be*, by Jack Canfield.

Matthew opened the book to the first section, "Take 100% Responsibility for Your Life," and read the following words:

> One of the most pervasive myths in American culture today is that we are *entitled* to a great life—that somehow, somewhere, someone (certainly not us) is responsible for filling our lives with continual happiness, exciting career options, nurturing family time, and blissful personal relationships simply because we exist.
>
> But the real truth—and the one lesson this whole book is based on—is that there is only one person responsible for the quality of the life you live.
>
> That person is *you*.

If you want to be successful, you must take 100% responsibility for everything that you experience in your life. This includes the level of your achievements, the results you produce, the quality of your relationships, the state of your health and physical fitness, your income, your debts, your feelings—everything!

This is not easy.

In fact, most of us have been conditioned to blame something outside ourselves for the parts of our life we don't like. We blame our parents, our bosses, our friends, the media, our coworkers, our clients, our spouse, the weather, the economy, our astrological chart, our lack of money—anyone or anything we can pin the blame on. We never want to look at where the real problem is—ourselves.

Each time Matthew read the book, it was like he was reading these words for the first time.

"BE responsible," Matthew said aloud.

9

Meetings, Meetings, and More Meetings!

Matthew sat at his desk reflecting on his meeting with Ms. Graves, and although it hadn't gone as well as he'd hoped, he was particularly excited about two other meetings on his calendar later in the afternoon. He was scheduled to have a discussion with his new assistant principal, Ms. Reeves, as well as his secretary, Ms. Rally. These were two key positions that would help him organize the staff and get everyone aligned. Ms. Rally seemed to be efficient and surely knew the school in and out—she had been with Mercy for over twenty years, serving multiple principals—so Matthew thought she would be a great asset to him. She managed the budget, set up work orders, and oversaw substitutes and teachers' absences. Not to mention he had witnessed many staff members entering her office and closing the door behind them, so he was pretty sure she had developed close connections with them, which he hoped to do as well.

The next meeting on his calendar was quickly approaching. He was meeting with Ms. Shields, Ms. Graves's comrade, who also left the faculty meeting at Ms. Graves's prompting. He really wanted to get out of his office and visit classrooms, but he knew he needed to address her behavior as he had with Ms. Graves. He planned to give her an opportunity to voice her concerns and set forth the expectations moving forward.

The meeting with Ms. Shields lasted a good ten minutes. She didn't have questions and even apologized for her behavior. Matthew could tell she was not one to be confrontational, but he also knew that he couldn't afford not to have a conversation about her conduct, especially as he was trying to transform the culture.

He followed up with an email to Ms. Shields as he did with Ms. Graves, summarizing the conversation so that all new expectations moving forward were clear. He shut down his computer and immediately began to prepare for classroom visits.

Matthew pulled his three-tiered metal rolling cart from the closet, which he had used at his last school, and placed his laptop, cell phone, and a pencil and pad on top—he called this his traveling office. The students and teachers at his last school loved having him in their classrooms and knew that whenever he pulled out his cart, they could probably expect a visit.

Matthew grabbed his last bit of cold coffee from earlier that morning to keep him inspired during his visits. As soon as he was done preparing his cart, however, his mission was interrupted by a soft knock at the door.

"Yes, come in," Matthew replied, anxious to see the unexpected visitor. He had become accustomed to visitors at his previous school and was often greeted by teachers who shared good things happening in their classrooms or by others needing helpful advice to remedy a situation. Even though he was anxious to get into classrooms, Matthew found it nice to hear the knock again.

"Good morning, Mr. Mason!" It was Ms. Helena, the art teacher. She popped through the door with her hair pulled back in a bun and a pencil tucked behind her ear, the same hairstyle she'd sported for as long as Matthew had known her. She wore a bright-yellow turtleneck sweater and a neon-green skirt that reached the floor. Ms. Helena was always in bright colors and unique patterns and sometimes even wore designs on her shirt that had nothing to do with her bottoms. It was like she pulled together her outfits in complete darkness, but for Ms. Helena, it was her own distinctive style.

"Good morning, how are you?!" Matthew replied, moving his attention away from her vibrant clothing and back to the purpose of her visit. "To what do I owe the pleasure of this visit?"

"Well, I know you're busy, so I'm not going to take up too much of your time, but I wanted to see if I could get some time on your calendar this week. I was so inspired by our faculty meeting yesterday and had some ideas on how our special-areas team could help you transform the culture here," Ms. Helena said with a big smile on her face. "We know that there will need to be a culture shift if true transformation is going to take place," she added.

"That would be awesome—I would love to speak with you about that," Matthew responded. Although it was clear that some of the faculty were enthusiastic about reforming the school, Matthew never expected anyone to step forward on their own and take initiative. He stood tall next to his traveling office with his shoulders held high, fueled by her incredible energy and support. Matthew thought to himself how much better the school would be if more teachers had the same attitude as Ms. Helena.

"We don't want you to become discouraged as you walk through the classrooms. There are some good things happening here, and good people too; it's just that the negativity is loud right now. Many of us have been waiting for a leader to help save our dear school, and after hearing you speak at the faculty meeting yesterday, we know that leader is you!" Ms.

Helena exclaimed gleefully. She clapped her hands together quietly, leaving them in a praying position for several seconds.

"I don't know what to say. I-I'm honored," Matthew stuttered, taken aback by her support. He opened his laptop to review his calendar. He knew that, in the future, he would need teachers to schedule time with him through Ms. Rally, but he was so encouraged by Ms. Helena's willingness to help that he didn't think it would be wise to turn her away.

"Does this same time work for you tomorrow?" Matthew asked.

"Yes, sir, this is my conference period," Ms. Helena responded, her attention drifting elsewhere. She was now staring at the cup of coffee that graced Matthew's cart.

"Great! I'll see you tomorrow!" Matthew confirmed, setting the meeting up on his calendar. His focus was on his computer, so he was too busy to notice that her mind had moved on to something else.

"BE responsible, huh?" Ms. Helena said softly to herself. The words made her pause and think about them longer. Matthew looked up with a confused expression as he processed her comment.

"Your coffee cup," Ms. Helena clarified, pointing to the cup before he could respond.

"Oh, yes, I had the opportunity to visit the Cup of Peace coffee shop this morning and just noticed a new message on the cup," Matthew explained. "Now, that place is special," he added.

"I've never been there, but I must pay it a visit, especially if they're giving out free advice," Ms. Helena chuckled, still staring at the cup. "That's what I want to talk to you about tomorrow. I love how you got us thinking yesterday about what we wanted to *BE*. I heard many teachers talking about it in the teacher's lounge yesterday, in a positive way."

Matthew was happy to hear that the teachers were touched by the vision exercise, and he couldn't wait to hear Ms. Helena's ideas. The more teachers he could get on his bus, the better.

"If we're going to change this school, we first must *BE*," Ms. Helena explained, looking at Matthew over her shoulder as she headed for the door. "Have a positive day, Mr. Mason, and remember: *BE*!"

"I love it! See you tomorrow, Ms. Helena," Matthew gasped excitedly as she left his office. He couldn't believe how much impact this one word was having on him and now on his team.

<hr />

Matthew stared at the *BE* poster on the wall and was reminded of the power of the word. The state of existing, being alive, being present: before the team could dive into any of the action items on their vision board, they had to first *BE*. As he stared at the vision poster, he wondered how he would possibly get them there. It seemed that many of the staff were so focused on Mercy's challenges that they missed the opportunity to use their existing talents to revive the school.

Matthew grabbed his traveling office and followed Ms. Helena's energy into the hallway. His own energy seemed to be contagious as he walked into classrooms. Many students waved at him, now that he had introduced himself at the assembly. This warmed his heart and was one of the bright spots in his day.

As he entered each classroom, Matthew tried to be as sensitive as possible, often walking over to say hello to the teacher first and pointing out something good that he observed. This seemed to lower the teacher's anxiety, allowing them to be a little more receptive to his visit. Matthew made it a point to enter the classroom with nothing in hand so that he could be fully present with the students and teachers. He took his notes about his visit *after* leaving the classroom. The goal was not to do a gotcha but to truly understand how they could improve teaching and learning.

After visiting several classrooms, Matthew decided to return to his office and reflect on his observations. He noted that teachers who worked on the same grade level didn't seem to collaborate; each teacher was teaching different content. Matthew's philosophy was that *what* we teach is the same, but *how* we teach it is up to the individual teacher. He had not observed consistent learning objectives, which made him wonder how teachers would be able to determine whether students had achieved the desired outcomes. The only classroom that had expectations for behavior was Ms. Helena's art classroom. He knew that if things were going to get better, there would need to be an alignment with teaching strategies and other practices.

Matthew shook his head as he wrote down what seemed to be the running theme throughout the school: teachers working in isolation. If he was ever going to address instruction, the staff would first need to know that he cared just as much about them as he did about getting results for the school; therefore, building connections was critical. Many of the staff were still feeling the pain of the last principal's departure, and several of them felt it was a punishment even to be associated with Mercy, so helping to change that perception and boosting morale were high priorities on his to-do list.

The good news was that Mercy's overall trouble was not reflected in every classroom. Some classrooms had great teaching and learning techniques that he was sure he could use as an example for other classrooms and build upon for even further improvement.

He had already sent out an email inviting teachers and staff to sign up for their one-on-ones, which he referred to as "Reflection Meetings." He planned to review expectations and allow each team member's voice to be heard by posing questions about their hopes and dreams for the new year. He had Ms. Rally create the sign-up sheet, which was almost completely filled, with the exception of the same folks who were openly hopeless regarding Mercy's future—most notably, Ms. Graves and Ms. Shields. But Matthew couldn't focus all his energy on the ones who were not on board; he knew that would only slow down his progress. His plan was to acknowledge and give his attention to the ones ready to move the school forward, because he was sure this would give their mission more energy.

The amount of work still left to be done was formidable, but he found it comforting that some parts of the school retained the spark that he remembered when he had taught here several years ago. He put away his observations and turned his attention to responding to emails, returning a few calls, and preparing for his meeting with the new assistant principal, Ms. Reeves. It was amazing to Matthew how quickly the time passed after he had knocked off a few items on his hope-to-do list. He had arrived early to accomplish several things, only to realize that there was not enough time in the day to do all the things he wanted.

Even though it was only his first week, Matthew knew he couldn't allow one day to pass without planning for the future. The building was filled with irreplaceable memories, and the thought of Mercy closing wasn't an option for him anymore.

Fueled by his determination, he grabbed his traveling office cart and headed toward the assistant principal's office for his next meeting.

10

BE Aware

"Knock, knock," he whispered, slowly opening the door to Ms. Reeves's office. To his surprise, Ms. Reeves was not alone. There was a young student sitting on the floor in the corner of her office with his head buried between his legs.

"Hi, Mr. Mason—sorry, I have an unexpected visitor. He has refused to move for the past twenty minutes," Ms. Reeves said, glancing over at the child. "Please come in and have a seat." She stood up to greet her new principal. Matthew went over and knelt down to the student's level and asked his name. The student stayed silent, keeping his head buried in his lap, never looking up to make eye contact.

"That's Jeremiah. He's a second grader here at Mercy," Ms. Reeves explained with an apologetic smile.

"My name is not Jeremiah!" the student shouted, lifting his head briefly before burying it again in his lap.

"Well, what *is* your name?" Matthew asked, still kneeling at the child's eye level.

"My name is JJ," the student responded, his voice muffled.

"JJ! That's a cool name," Matthew said, trying to engage with the student. "So I see you're crying, JJ. Are you sad?"

"No, I'm mad!" JJ shouted from underneath his arms, drawing his knees in even closer.

"Okay, I can see you're mad. Can you tell me what you're mad about?" Matthew asked in a calm, caring voice.

"My teacher is mean! She wouldn't let me eat my snack, and I'm hungry," JJ exclaimed, still avoiding eye contact.

"So you're mad because your teacher wouldn't allow you to eat your snack. Is that right?" Matthew said, checking for understanding.

"Yeah, I'm mad!" JJ yelled again, now kicking his foot against a chair that was placed next to him.

Ms. Reeves could not believe that the student was having a conversation. When his teacher had called for assistance, she and the counselor, Ms. Love, had to physically pick JJ up and carry him into her office because he had refused to stand up and walk.

Neither she nor Ms. Love had been able to engage him in a conversation because he had shut down and refused to talk. The teacher had summoned them, she said, because he was interrupting valuable instruction time by refusing to do his work.

"I understand you're mad about not being able to eat your snack," Matthew continued, making sure he provided JJ with physical space. "What have you tried?"

Matthew had always been interested in student behavior and had worked with other leaders in his previous district on de-escalation techniques. He was aware of his physical proximity and how it could escalate a student's behavior. He wanted to get on JJ's level so that his posture did not appear threatening or dominant.

After a few seconds of wait time and no response, Matthew asked again: "I understand you're mad about not being able to eat your snack. Can you tell me what you've tried?"

"Nothing! My teacher is mean!" JJ exclaimed.

"What *can you* try?" Matthew probed delicately, still trying to get the student to think of an action he could take.

"I told her I was hungry, and she said I had to wait till lunch," the student explained, finally looking up and turning to stare directly out the window.

"Okay, so you tried telling your teacher that you were hungry. How did that work for you?" Matthew questioned.

"It didn't! She's mean!" JJ yelled again.

"Okay. What else can you try?" Matthew asked, patiently waiting for JJ to respond.

Still gazing out the window, JJ was quiet for several seconds. His breathing had visibly slowed down, and he appeared to be calmer and less anxious.

"I guess I could write her a note," JJ replied finally, looking into Matthew's eyes.

"That's a good idea!" Matthew agreed, his face lighting up in response to the student's active participation.

"What else can you try?" Matthew probed again. He looked at the child kindly to avoid pressuring him.

"I guess I could try asking her nicely?" JJ asked.

"These are awesome ideas! Think about what you will say in your letter to your teacher, and we'll get you something to write with," Matthew said.

Matthew confirmed his understanding of JJ's intention and provided encouragement. "So you're going to write your letter and ask your teacher nicely about eating your snack, right? Once you've done that, can you come back and let us know how it worked for you?" Matthew finally stood up straight, hoping to get JJ to do the same.

"Who is your teacher?" Matthew asked curiously.

"Ms. Graves," the student responded reluctantly, finally wiping the tears from his face and sitting up. Matthew closed his eyes for a second as he released a low exhale.

"Stay here. I'm going to grab some paper so that you can write Ms. Graves that letter," Matthew said, heading toward the door.

"Wait, I have paper," Ms. Reeves chimed in, trying to save Matthew an unnecessary trip.

"Oh, no, I have special paper in my office," Matthew responded, giving Ms. Reeves a wink to indicate he had something else to take care of. Matthew went to his office and tore a sheet of paper from his notebook. The paper had yellow stars at the top, and he was sure JJ would love it. Matthew dropped the paper off with Ms. Reeves, who was now sitting with JJ, and proceeded to walk down the hall to visit with Ms. Graves.

Matthew said a quick prayer before knocking on Ms. Graves's classroom door. He entered immediately, before she invited him in. Ms. Graves was eating at the guided reading table at the back of the classroom, while her students were sitting on the floor watching a cartoon. Ms. Graves jumped up at the sight of her new principal, wiped her mouth with a napkin, and quickly placed her carrots back into her Tupperware container.

Matthew walked over to the table to greet Ms. Graves and informed her that he had spoken with JJ, who was with the assistant principal. He asked Ms. Graves to share what had happened to land JJ in the principal's office.

"Look, these kids can't do whatever they want. He was trying to eat crackers in front of the other kids. I told him he had to wait until lunch, and he refused," Ms. Graves said, moving away from the guided reading table and over to her desk in an attempt to take Matthew's attention away from the snacks she was eating.

"So you have a 'no eating' policy in your classroom?" Matthew asked, staring back at the Tupperware container on the guided reading table.

"Look! I'm not a child. They don't get to do what I do," Ms. Graves responded in a snappy tone.

"Ms. Graves, if a child is expressing that they're hungry, don't you think we need to take time to investigate to see if they've eaten? We know that many of our kids come to school without having eaten the night before," Matthew reminded her firmly.

"Isn't that a personal problem?" Ms. Graves scoffed, looking directly into Matthew's eyes.

Being aware of and sensitive to students' needs was a bare minimum for teachers, so Ms. Graves's attitude only further upset Matthew. However, to remain professional, he kept his cool and modeled the communication techniques he expected to see in every person on campus. *BE*, Matthew thought to himself. He knew that he would not be able to address the issue at this moment, as he was also witnessing students watching cartoons during instructional time.

"Ms. Graves, students' problems become our problem the moment they step into the school. Now, JJ is going to return to class to speak with you about having a snack. The expectation is that you will listen to him and help him come up with a good plan to have his snack. Do you understand?" Matthew asked.

"Sure. You know your plan is not going to work here, right?" Ms. Graves said, reminding Matthew that she didn't believe in his mission to save Mercy.

"It will work as long as we believe it will, Ms. Graves," Matthew retorted.

Before leaving, Matthew had to address the students seated on the floor watching cartoons.

"By the way, I reviewed your lesson plans for the week, and I don't recall anything about watching cartoons. Could you explain?" Matthew asked, turning his attention to the students.

"Look, I had some other work to do since you refused to allow us to leave the meeting yesterday. I bet I'm not the only one showing cartoons today. I tried to warn you!" Ms. Graves snapped.

"Please turn that off and engage your students in productive learning," Matthew advised. He was beginning to think that Ms. Graves was Mercy's biggest problem and the reason they couldn't move forward.

Matthew called Ms. Reeves on his walkie-talkie and asked her to help JJ finish his letter and requested that she escort him back to his classroom when it was done. Matthew thought it would be a good idea for him to wait and observe the interaction between JJ and Ms. Graves to make sure she responded in a positive way. Ms. Graves walked over to her computer and shut down the cartoon students were watching.

"Aw, man!" several students exclaimed in dismay.

"Get to your seats, and let's do some work," Ms. Graves directed the students, giving Matthew a hard stare.

When JJ arrived with Ms. Reeves by his side, he handed Ms. Graves the note he had written. She honored his request to eat his snack in Ms. Reeves's office, away from the other students.

Matthew informed Ms. Graves that he would schedule another meeting with her to discuss today's incident. Although Ms. Graves's behavior had drained his energy, he picked himself up and started his journey back to Ms. Reeves's office. In his heart he knew that this was headed toward a growth plan for Ms. Graves, but he would need to gather more information to determine the areas for development. Right now, it was simply too much.

Matthew used to believe that attitude was 90 percent of what we do each day. After his encounters with Ms. Graves, he now realized that it was 110 percent of everything we do. How can I help her grow her attitude? he asked himself.

Ms. Graves didn't seem to be aware of how her negative attitude was impacting others, especially the young students she worked with. *BE* aware, he thought to himself.

Matthew was starting to see how they could begin shaping the values, attitudes, and behaviors for Mercy with the power of *BE*...

11

BE Open

Matthew returned to his office and quickly sent Ms. Graves an email inviting her to meet with him and Ms. Reeves after school to discuss his observations in her classroom. He made sure she received the message by having Ms. Rally walk down to her classroom to inform her of the meeting.

Matthew returned to Ms. Reeves's office to brief her on what he had observed in Ms. Graves's classroom and to inform her that she would need to be a part of the meeting after school. Since this would be his second time meeting with Ms. Graves, he thought it was important to have a witness present.

Matthew tried to turn his attention to his originally scheduled meeting with Ms. Reeves, but he was having a difficult time concentrating after what he had just experienced. He felt horrible that his and Ms. Reeves's time together had been interrupted, but he wanted to use the time they had left to learn more about her experiences while also sharing how she could support him moving forward. It was important to Matthew that he and Ms. Reeves worked together as a team. He wanted her to shadow him as much as possible to ensure she didn't get lost in all the negativity.

Ms. Reeves couldn't wait to meet with her new principal. This was her first assistant principal position, and she wanted to do a good job. She had heard a lot about Matthew from Superintendent Rodriguez when she was hired, and she knew she could learn a lot from his leadership.

Ms. Reeves realized that their meeting would be cut short because they had to spend a great deal of time getting JJ settled back into the classroom. So, when he asked her to tell him how and why she became an educator, she didn't waste any time jumping in.

"I've been in education for over ten years now. I enjoyed playing teacher as a young girl and loved reading and teaching my younger siblings. I'm the oldest of five kids, and all my sisters and brothers are in the medical field," she shared with a smile. "I was headed down the same path, but then I had the opportunity to intern in an elementary school. I was so inspired by watching teachers work with students and seeing the impact they had on kids' lives that I changed my path immediately. My parents were not too happy with my decision, but I've always been encouraged by my mentors to be open to finding my own truth." Ms. Reeves shared her thoughts quickly, as if she was running out of time.

"BE open," Matthew repeated with a smile.

"Yes, when you're open, you are welcoming the possibilities. You don't close yourself off or limit yourself. You're open to opportunities," Ms. Reeves said with a glowing smile. "By the way, I loved your vision exercise yesterday, when you asked the team what they wanted Mercy to *BE*. I saw a lot of faces in deep thought during that exercise."

"That's great to hear. I'm meeting with Ms. Helena, the art teacher, tomorrow, to discuss some of her ideas related to the vision exercise," Matthew shared. "If you're not busy, I would love for you to share your thoughts with her on what it means to BE open, as you've shared with me today."

"I would BE honored," Ms. Reeves said with a thoughtful laugh, changing her tone to emphasize the word *BE*.

"So how did you end up in the city of Grace?" Matthew asked, trying to finish up their conversation.

"My husband got a new job, so we had to relocate to Grace. Luckily Mercy needed a new assistant principal at the same time, so it kind of seemed like fate to me." Ms. Reeves chuckled lightly as she rocked excitedly in her seat. "One of the most important things to me is making sure that everyone's voice is equally heard. Of course, I understand it's impossible to please everyone, but at least listening to and acknowledging the needs of our team, from students to teachers to families, should be a priority. We can't build a positive school environment if we focus only on our scores," Ms. Reeves explained, her eyes lit with passion.

Matthew found himself nodding along in agreement with many of Ms. Reeves's comments. As important as pleasing the district and state were in determining Mercy's fate, raising student scores and improving teaching skills weren't going to be enough if people didn't enjoy coming to work.

Ms. Reeves seemed to agree that building a positive culture would be essential to Mercy's success. She exhibited a calm and caring energy that gave Matthew even more hope that she would be a great asset to him in leading Mercy's turnaround. She appeared to be the perfect assistant to drive their new initiatives. A weight started to lift from his shoulders as he felt even more confident in her ability to lead.

He explained to Ms. Reeves that there might be times when the staff would treat them like Mom and Pop, especially in a school with a toxic culture that is undergoing a lot of change. When they didn't get their way from one "parent," they might test the relationship by going to the other one and asking the same question. He explained plainly how important it would be that they were unified as a leadership team. He told her that if she ever disagreed with him about something or needed to vent, his door would always be open. However, it needed to happen behind closed doors and not in the presence of the staff. He and Ms. Reeves needed to show a united front.

Ms. Reeves agreed and appreciated Matthew taking the time to explain his expectations. She had been in schools where the leaders didn't take the time to communicate and would become upset when she did something that didn't align with their uncommunicated ideals, so she loved the fact that Matthew was clear about what he needed. She was already feeling comfortable and impressed by her new leader.

Matthew was also pleased with Ms. Reeves's philosophy and her willingness to be open to learning and growing along the way. Ms. Reeves expressed that she would one day like to lead her own school and was happy to hear that Matthew would support her in doing so.

"I don't hire assistant principals, you know," Matthew said with a big smile. "Only future principals."

"Hey, one more question before you leave," Ms. Reeves said in a serious voice. "How did you do that?"

"Do what?" Matthew asked curiously, stopping short of exiting her office.

"That thing you did with JJ! That was amazing!" Ms. Reeves exclaimed, giving him a thumbs-up.

"Oh, that's a technique I learned years ago. It's called the SAMA method. It's a de-escalation training I went through when I was first hired to be a teacher," Matthew explained, feeling good about his breakthrough with little JJ. "It works not only with children, you know, but with adults too."

"You'll have to teach that to me one day," said Ms. Reeves, nodding her head vigorously to acknowledge the effectiveness of the process.

"I would be delighted to!" Matthew replied with a smile. "You just need to remember one thing."

"Yeah, what's that?" Ms. Reeves asked. Her eyes shone with curiosity about what Matthew would say next.

"BE open," he said with a smile.

"Oh, yeah, I can definitely do that," she said, returning the smile.

12

Meet Ms. Rally

At the end of the day, Matthew's goal for Mercy was bigger than just saving it from closure. He wanted to ensure that the school was put back on track to become one of the top schools in the district and the community. Matthew took great pride in treating students and teachers as the leaders of their own lives, and that's what he was committed to modeling for the entire staff.

He didn't want Mercy just to be as good as it was before; he wanted it to be better. He dreamed of a school where teachers and students were excited to come every day and learn something new. Even though the journey was not going to be easy, Matthew had to make sure he remembered never to allow any limiting beliefs to sabotage his plans. It was easy to become discouraged by the things he was seeing with his own eyes, so he had to rely on his mental vision to paint a picture of what things could be. He believed that with the right attitude and beliefs, there was no limit to what the team could accomplish.

Remembering that he had a meeting scheduled with Ms. Rally, Matthew moved past his thoughts and immediately began to prepare for his discussion with his secretary.

Looking up toward the door to his office, he saw that Ms. Rally had been standing outside waiting to enter. She clutched a notepad that she held close to her heart. The clock on his cell phone showed that he was a few minutes late for their meeting, so he apologized for his tardiness and invited her inside.

Although Matthew was exhausted, he thought it was important to keep his commitments with his staff, especially since they were still getting to know him as a new leader. He couldn't believe that it was almost time for school to let out and teachers would be preparing for dismissal soon. Matthew wanted to at least start a conversation with Ms. Rally, but he also knew it would be important to observe the school's dismissal process. Again he would need to end the meeting early with Ms. Rally if he wanted to get to dismissal on time. *BE*, he thought to himself.

He pulled up a chair and invited Ms. Rally to have a seat next to him. He had worked with her when he was a teacher and remembered how kind and helpful she was to him then. Today he noticed her energy was a bit cold; she stared at him as if she were conducting a walk-through. Matthew had never noticed this behavior from Ms. Rally before, but then he remembered that he had not had the opportunity to sit with her one-on-one since he had been named principal.

"It's so good to work with you again, Ms. Rally! I still remember how helpful you were to me when I first started teaching. You taught me how to create a plan to get funds from our PTO for new laptops. Remember that?" Matthew said, hoping to remind Ms. Rally of their previous relationship.

"Good to see you too," Ms. Rally responded with no emotion, as if the words meant nothing. She opened her notepad to an empty page, holding her pen like a weapon she was waiting to use.

"Well, I apologize again for my tardiness. Ms. Reeves and I were dealing with a student issue that took a little longer than we expected. I'll plan on scheduling more time for us to meet later this week, since I will need to head out to observe dismissal soon. Is that okay?" Matthew asked the question politely as a form of courtesy; however, he knew Ms. Rally did not have a real choice in the matter.

"That's fine," Ms. Rally replied, her eyes buried in her notepad, showing little interest in their conversation.

"The reason I wanted to meet was to understand your role and how I can support you as we transform the culture here," Matthew said, leaning forward for a more casual approach. He could tell there was awkwardness and tension swimming in the air, but he couldn't put his finger on why this was happening. *BE*, Matthew reminded himself, taking a deep breath and glancing at the vision poster that hung directly over Ms. Rally's head.

"So you want to see how you can support me, huh?" Ms. Rally said with a sarcastic chuckle.

"Well, realistically speaking, we will be supporting one another, but I thought it was important that we meet so that I can understand exactly what your responsibilities are," Matthew continued with a forced smile, hoping to get past the discomfort and find common ground.

"First, I'm the secretary, and I don't just work for you—my job is to support the teachers and staff too. I've been doing this work for twenty years without any help, and that's the way I would prefer to keep it. I don't need some new person coming in and trying to change everything and getting me..."

"Hold on," Matthew said calmly, interrupting Ms. Rally. He could tell she was anxious and wanted to see if he could calm her down and change the direction of the conversation.

"Ms. Rally, this meeting is a chance for us to talk about how we will work together. I know that there are many systems in place that I'm not familiar with, and I'll need your help in understanding what those are as I get started. Does that make sense?" he asked, still hoping to jump-start a productive conversation.

Matthew glanced again at the *BE* poster, a reminder of the vision for Mercy. If he was going to change the culture of the school, he would need to help the staff move past their fears so that they had the courage to do the work that needed to be done. This could not happen if he was not able to build trusting connections.

His thoughts were suspended by the sound of Ms. Rally's voice. "Well, I supported Dr. Thomas for ten years. I helped manage his calendar, answered his calls, returned many of the calls he didn't want to be bothered with, managed the budget—which we will need to discuss since many of the funds we were allocated were spent prior to you coming. I also manage teacher absences and make sure they have substitutes to cover classes. That's just *a few* of the things I do," she explained with a stoic expression, never cracking a smile. Ms. Rally kept her chin up and spoke with an air of confidence, as if she ruled the schoolyard.

"Okay, that really helps," Matthew said, nodding his head and making notes in his own notebook. He knew what it felt like to have someone new come in and make a lot of changes without bothering to figure out what was already working. He had experienced that with many of the leaders he worked with.

"Helps what?" Ms. Rally countered.

"Helps me understand how you can support me as I get started," Matthew said with a smile. He wanted to make sure that they had a clear understanding of each other's roles and responsibilities, especially since they would be working so closely together.

"I would like to meet at least once a week to go over anything you think you need to share with me to keep me posted regarding budgeting, purchases, subs, or anything else, for that matter. What do you think?" Matthew asked, trying to give Ms. Rally the opportunity to voice her opinion.

"Fine with me. You're the boss!" Ms. Rally said, slamming down her pen.

Matthew slowly closed his notebook and asked, "What's going on, Ms. Rally? You've been very short during our meeting. I want us to have a good working relationship, but as you know, a relationship takes two. Please share with me what you're feeling right now." Matthew then allowed time for Ms. Rally to respond.

Caught off guard by his candidness, Ms. Rally closed her notepad with the pen still nestled inside and shared with Matthew how nervous she was about all the changes happening so quickly. She expressed how much she loved Mercy and wanted to protect it with all she had, but she was worried that Mercy would eventually close and she would be out of a job.

Matthew paused for a moment, leaving space to appreciate Ms. Rally's honesty. He didn't want to interrupt the silence so quickly that her words would not have a chance to linger in the air.

"Ms. Rally, take a look behind you," Matthew finally said, pointing the *BE* poster. "If we're going to make this vision our reality, we're going to have to work together. My goal is to understand each person's strengths and talents and how we can apply them to save Mercy. I'm not here to change things but to transform the things we've been doing so that they work to turn Mercy into the learning environment we all know it can be. And I need your help, Ms. Rally." Matthew smiled warmly.

For the first time during the meeting, Ms. Rally smiled, a tear rolling down her cheek. No words were needed; the room was now filled with less friction, as if someone had opened a window.

Ms. Rally thanked Matthew for his time and reminded him that dismissal was starting soon. She turned to exit the office, holding on to her notepad and a smile.

Before grabbing his jacket and walkie-talkie to head out for dismissal, Matthew looked up toward the ceiling and whispered a soft thank-you to the heavens for turning around the meeting with Ms. Rally. After observing what had happened in Ms. Graves's classroom, he didn't know if his plate had room for one more attitude. He had already been served! He rushed into the hallway to say his goodbyes to students and observe the dismissal.

13

BE Courageous

M atthew stood in awe watching the kids as they went their various ways to return home. He was always so impressed with the school dismissal process. The teachers and staff were great at sorting through all the complexities of bus riders, car riders, walkers, and day-care riders. It was enough to make your head spin. But eventually the crowd of students dwindled down to a handful in the front office waiting for transportation that had not arrived or for their parents to be called. Matthew didn't observe anything out of the ordinary with dismissal but did note ways that the process could be made more efficient.

After dismissal Matthew retreated to his office, closed the door, and kicked his feet up on his desk. He rested his head inside the palms of his hands as he leaned back into his reclining seat. He was expecting Ms. Reeves and Ms. Graves to arrive shortly for their meeting to talk about the incident with JJ and students watching cartoons during instructional time, but he wanted to clear his mind a bit before they arrived.

There was no need to prepare for this meeting; he simply wanted to understand why Ms. Graves thought it was okay to eat in front of students when they weren't allowed to eat in the classroom, *and* he wanted her to explain the purpose of the cartoon the students were watching during instruction time.

He honestly didn't feel that his efforts to help Ms. Graves would change her attitude; she seemed to be stuck in her ways. However, he tried his best to remain optimistic. The meeting for him would be a way to gather more documentation so that he could make a decision about her future with Mercy.

He gazed out of the large window in his office and reflected on his day. While he hadn't gotten as much accomplished as he had hoped, he was excited about his meeting tomorrow with Ms. Helena. It would be great to talk about something positive for a change.

While his conversation with Ms. Rally did not start off well, it did end on a good note. He had a pleasant discussion with Ms. Reeves, and he was even able to get into a few classrooms and observe a few things that were going well in the building. All in all, it wasn't a bad day, he thought to himself.

Suddenly a knock at the door brought him back into the current moment. He immediately placed his feet back on the floor. "Yes, come in," he said in a loud tone to ensure his voice was heard. He stood up, expecting to greet Ms. Graves and Ms. Reeves for their meeting. But, to his surprise, it was Ms. Rally.

"A couple of parents are here to see you," she said in a concerned voice. "Their daughter didn't get off the bus this afternoon, and they're very worried."

"Oh, no!" Matthew exclaimed.

"Yes, and believe it or not, this has happened before. I'll call the bus barn to notify them. She's a first grader, and her parents are Mr. and Mrs. Porter," Ms. Rally said before turning away to resume the search.

Matthew's heart started pounding. He quickly straightened his suit jacket and tie and followed Ms. Rally's shadow into the reception area, where he found a middle-aged man and woman holding on to one another. He noticed that the woman was crying, and the man had a worried look on his face. "Where is our daughter?!" the man shouted as soon as Matthew turned the corner.

Matthew extended his hand to introduce himself, but neither the man nor the woman greeted him in return. Ms. Rally sat with the phone close to her ear, anxiously waiting to speak to the bus supervisor.

"Our daughter never got off the bus!" the man shouted at Matthew. "Where is our daughter?"

"Okay, we'll be happy to help. What's your daughter's name, and how does she usually get home?" Matthew asked, trying to remain calm.

"Oh my God!" the mother exclaimed, turning to her husband with tears rolling down her cheeks. "He doesn't even know who our daughter is; how can he help us?"

"Their daughter's name is Emma Porter, and she rides Bus 165," Ms. Rally said, looking away from her computer to provide Matthew with more information.

"Ms. Rally is contacting the bus supervisor now; we should know something soon," Matthew advised. "Who is her teacher?" Matthew asked the parents.

"Ms. Shields!" the mother shouted.

All of a sudden, Matthew felt a huge cramp in his stomach. He calmly picked up the intercom phone in the reception area, trying not to further upset the parents. "Ms. Shields to the front office, please. Ms. Shields to the front office," he announced in a calm voice.

The phone rang a few seconds later. It was one of the teachers across the hall from Ms. Shields, who informed Matthew that Ms. Shields had already left for the day. Matthew glanced at the clock. It was only 3:46 p.m. Teachers were not scheduled to leave until 4:00 p.m., and he had not received any notification that she would be leaving school early.

While Ms. Rally was on the phone with the bus supervisor, Ms. Reeves had heard the commotion and came to the reception area to see what was going on. Matthew gave her a brief account of the situation, and Ms. Reeves immediately jumped in to help.

"Let me give Ms. Shields a call on her cell phone," Ms. Reeves suggested. She went back to her office to make the call.

"Do you think Emma would have gotten off the bus with a friend?" Matthew asked the parents, who were becoming visibly more and more upset as they observed all the activities aimed at locating their missing child.

"No! Why would she do that?!" the father shouted back at Matthew.

"I'm only trying to help. I just want to make sure we explore all avenues. That's all," Matthew said, still trying to calm the parents.

Matthew wanted to remove the parents, tuck them away in another room so that he could take full charge of the situation without them being his audience. However, he knew that he would have a difficult time asking the parents to sit anywhere, especially away from the scene.

"The bus supervisor is calling the bus driver now and will let us know when he's gotten in touch with him," Ms. Rally reported.

"Great! Let me see if Ms. Reeves has gotten in touch with Ms. Shields." Matthew left the reception area and walked into Ms. Reeves's office. He needed to remove himself from the parents' view for a moment. He didn't want them to see how nervous he really was.

Matthew felt like his heart was going to jump out of his chest. Remembering he had the handkerchief in his pocket from the day before, he grabbed it and dabbed the sweat that was now forming above his brows. How could a child be missing? If God was trying to run him off the job, this was definitely the way to do it.

As he entered Ms. Reeves's office, he found her on the phone with Ms. Shields, who was already home. Ms. Graves was standing by his office door with the same angry look she wore during their first meeting.

"Sorry, Ms. Graves, we will have to postpone our meeting until tomorrow. We've had something important come up," he explained.

"I knew this was going to happen. If something is going to go wrong, it's going to happen at Mercy," Ms. Graves said.

"Ms. Graves, could you kindly leave? Right now we need to stay as calm and positive as possible, and I can't listen to any negative comments right now," Matthew said sternly.

"Excuse me," Ms. Graves said as she walked away slowly, starring back at Matthew.

Matthew quickly turned his attention back to the missing child and joined Ms. Reeves in her office. "Did Emma get on the bus?" Ms. Reeves asked Ms. Shields over the phone.

Matthew stood by the phone trying to figure out what Ms. Shields was saying. He could hardly concentrate, thinking about the little girl and praying and hoping she was safe. Ms. Reeves placed the receiver down on her desk and put the phone on speaker so that Matthew could listen to the conversation.

Matthew was deeply impressed by Ms. Reeves's professionalism and her ability to be so calm when it seemed like the building was on fire and falling apart. It took a lot of courage for her to jump in and help take charge of the situation.

"I think she got on the bus. Hold on. Let me think," Ms. Shields responded nervously.

Matthew wanted to ask her why she had left school early, but he felt this was not the time for that. All he wanted was to make sure that the student was placed on the bus. At this time Ms. Shields couldn't even guarantee that.

"Hi, Ms. Shields, it's Mr. Mason!" Matthew said interrupting their conversation. "Do you have a log of students and their modes of transportation?" he asked.

"No one asked us to do that! We've never done that before. Kids know where they're supposed to go," Ms. Shields replied anxiously.

"I'm trying to understand your system for tracking students. That's all," Matthew said.

"Well, I'm sorry. I don't remember if she got on the bus or not," said Ms. Shields.

Matthew could not believe what he was hearing. A teacher leaves school without ensuring that all her students are safe, and now, knowing that one of her students is missing, simply apologizes and hangs up the phone. Boy, do I have my work cut out for me, Matthew thought.

Suddenly Ms. Rally appeared in the doorway and said, "Emma just showed up!"

"Where?!" Matthew said as he and Ms. Reeves made their way back to the reception area.

As they entered the rotunda, they found the Porters consoling their daughter while another woman stood over them, smiling with joy.

"Hi, Mr. Mason. I'm Ms. Johnson, Jeffrey's mom," the woman said, extending her hand to shake Matthew's.

"What happened?" Matthew said, never acknowledging the warm greeting.

"Well, I was coming down Highway 6 and saw a little girl crossing the busy roadway. It just didn't look safe to me—she looked scared and lost. When I noticed she was wearing a backpack that said Mercy Elementary School, I immediately pulled over and approached the poor baby. I'm happy I did. It seems the bus driver had let her off at the wrong stop, and she was lost.

"I'm just happy I had my son Jeffrey in the car, because she didn't know me from Adam, and I could tell she became even more afraid when I pulled over to talk with her. She saw

Jeffrey, and she seemed to be relieved. She and Jeffrey have been in the same class since preschool," said Ms. Johnson.

"Oh my God, thank you for bringing her back," Matthew said, embracing Ms. Johnson in a hug. This was not normally how Matthew would greet a parent, but he was so relieved that the child had been found that he didn't know what else to do.

"I was happy to do it. That could have been a horrible situation. Plus, I would want someone to do it for my kid," Ms. Johnson responded.

After the Porters regained their composure, they thanked Ms. Johnson and then turned to Matthew to demand a better dismissal process. "How could you not know if all your students got on the bus or not?" the father said, staring at Matthew.

The parent was right. There needed to be more accountability and systems in place to make sure this type of incident didn't happen again. Matthew needed to know that he had staff who took this seriously and understood their role in ensuring the safety of their students. And apparently Ms. Shields didn't understand this, as she left school early instead of making sure her students were safe.

"Yes, I will meet with Ms. Shields and the bus driver tomorrow and make sure we have proper protocols in place so that this doesn't happen again," Matthew assured the parents.

Matthew thanked Ms. Johnson again for bringing the child to safety, and he reassured Mr. and Mrs. Porter that he would be looking into the situation thoroughly tomorrow. The problem was that he could not be totally sure it wouldn't happen again, because he had to rely on his teachers to make good decisions, and at this point, Matthew didn't trust the system he had just witnessed.

Matthew thanked Ms. Rally and Ms. Reeves for their help and for staying late to make sure Emma was safe. Then he didn't waste any more time talking or thinking. He went directly to his office, grabbed his backpack, and headed to his car.

Outside the building, he was greeted by a fresh breeze that whizzed across his face. This was exactly what he needed. He opened the back door to his car, removed his jacket (which was now drenched with sweat), and placed it on the back seat. He sat staring at the school for several moments, thanking God for bringing the child back to safety and wondering if he had made the right decision to return to Grace.

With his heart still racing from the incident, Matthew started the car and prepared to go to the one place he felt safe—home.

14

BE Grateful

The next morning Matthew woke up to one of the babies crying. He couldn't believe he had finally fallen asleep. He had tossed and turned all night after his stressful first day, and now it was time to do it all over again.

He was so grateful that little Emma was found and was safe at home with her parents. His mind couldn't help but imagine what would have happened if she had not been wearing that Mercy Elementary backpack and if that parent hadn't recognized her. It seemed that every time his mind drifted to the incident, his body would literally tremble just thinking about it.

He had a lot of meetings on his agenda today, and he didn't know how he would get to all of them. He pulled out his laptop and sent a quick message to Ms. Rally:

Good morning, Ms. Rally, Happy Wednesday!

First, thank you for meeting with me yesterday and being open about how we can become a stronger team. I also want to thank you for staying late to help with the bus situation. I appreciate you and am looking forward to a wonderful year.

I will need you to add a few meetings to my calendar today so that we can make sure we are keeping our students safe. Kindly look at my calendar and add the meetings below. Please include Ms. Reeves on all of these, if she's available:

- I need to meet with Ms. Shields and eventually the entire staff to ensure they have a process for knowing students' modes of transportation.

- Schedule meeting with the driver of Bus 165 to inquire about student drop-off procedures.

- Reschedule meeting with Ms. Graves and Ms. Reeves that was supposed to happen after school yesterday.

- Look at my calendar to see if I have time to meet with Ms. Helena during her conference period today.

Thanks for all you do,
Matthew

Matthew recognized that they needed to set expectations for the staff sooner rather than later. They would never get things on the right track and create a safe culture if they didn't have values to guide their behavior. It seemed that everyone was currently operating on their personal values and beliefs systems, which was one reason the culture was so toxic.

Before Baelor and Bella were born, Matthew and Samantha had a solid morning routine of self-care: exercising, meditation, affirmations, reading, and journaling. They had both read the book *The Miracle Morning*, by Hal Elrod, and had been inspired by his story to create their very own power hour. For a whole year, their morning consisted of a solid routine of self-care. They would get up early before work, and the routine seemed to help them throughout their day, especially when times got tough.

They tried to keep up with it, but with the babies and their busy work schedules, they had fallen off course. Matthew knew that if he was going to thrive in his new role, he would need to get back to embracing his miracle morning. He took the babies' crying as a sign from God to get up and resurrect his morning ritual.

Matthew dusted off his workout equipment in the garage for a quick workout and decided to read a few pages from Jack Welch's book *Winning*. He remembered reading the book years ago when he first started teaching, which really helped him create a positive classroom culture. This book was just the message Matthew needed to hear this morning as he was thinking about how to align his team.

In the first chapter, "Mission and Values," Welch writes that "a good mission statement and a good set of values are so real they smack you in the face with their concreteness. The mission announces exactly where you are going, and the values describe the behaviors that will get you there." Welch goes on to say that he prefers "abandoning the term *values* altogether in favor of just *behaviors*."

That was it! Matthew thought. They would need to be intentional about the behaviors they expected to see, not just in teachers but in students and families as well. If his team didn't have any concrete values (behaviors), then they would continue to support a mob-style culture in which each person was following their own personal values and beliefs.

Matthew couldn't wait to get to work. He knew he had a lot of meetings to get to, but he hoped he could meet with Ms. Helena because he saw her playing a valuable role in creating these value statements, and the word *BE* would play an important part in getting them started.

Matthew showered and quickly got dressed. He was energized and ready to get his team on the right track. He had not felt this alive since the day he found out he would be named principal. As he watched his three girls sleeping, he had a new reason to get this school functioning in a healthy direction: so that he wouldn't miss out on all their important milestones. Not to mention how much he missed spending time with his beautiful wife. He was so grateful that she had stayed up last night to hear about his day. She always reminded him that everything was in God's hands and that all would be fine.

Turning Mercy around was important to him, but he realized that being a good husband and father was even more important. *BE.* The word popped into his head almost as a reminder of how to begin his day. He had just finished his mediation, which he now knew was giving him practice in BEing. Being present, being mindful, celebrating being alive! It was such a powerful word that immediately put his mind and body at ease.

With only moments to spare, Matthew kissed his girls on the forehead and jetted out the door.

"Coffee, honey?" Samantha yelled, her voice trying to catch up with Matthew.

"Don't get up, sweetheart; I'll grab some on the way!" Matthew yelled over his shoulder before adding, "Love you!" Heading toward A Cup of Peace, he was anxious to see what he would learn this morning from his new favorite coffee shop.

As he drove out into the twilight, his headlights beamed so brightly that they seemed to act as his guardian angels, leading him down streets that were still covered with darkness. Here he was again, heading into the world of the unknown, not knowing what this day had in store for him. His power hour had filled his soul with a quiet sense of peace as he carried the word *BE* in his heart.

As he approached A Cup of Peace, he slowly pulled his sedan into the drive-thru and tried to savor his beautiful moment with the soothing music that played through the speaker. He glanced into his rearview mirror and couldn't understand why there was not a line of cars waiting to get a delicious cup of peace.

His thoughts were interrupted by the sound of Cindy's sweet voice, sounding as if she had been expecting him. "Good morning, Matthew! We're so happy you're here. Will you be having Angelic Americano, black?" she asked, her voice full of life.

"Aah, yes, please, I'll have the Angelic Americano, black," Matthew repeated, surprised that she knew he was there *and* that she remembered what he had had the day before. He felt like he was their only customer.

"We have a camera right at the top of the menu board, Matthew," Cindy said with a chuckle, as if she could read his mind.

Matthew's eyes immediately drifted to the top of the menu display board, where he noticed a green light staring back at him. He was happy to be aware that his every move was on display. He tilted his head and shared a bashful smile.

Matthew didn't waste any time pulling up to the window to greet Cindy and watch the employees' teamwork on display. His plan was to bring this same atmosphere to his school.

"Good morning! How are you today, Principal Mason?" Cindy asked.

Matthew couldn't remember if he had given Cindy his last name but imagined she could have learned it from the superintendent, since he had been bragging about Matthew taking the position at Mercy.

"I'm good! How are you, Ms. Cindy?" Matthew asked, trying to take the focus away from himself and handing the attention back to her.

"We're GREAT!" the team shouted in unison.

"We believe that we become what we think. And what we think impacts how we feel! So we're GREAT!" Cindy said, reinforcing the team's energy.

Matthew listened in awe. Cindy was serving much more than coffee: she was dropping knowledge. Who was this lady? He wanted to ask about the "BE..." messages printed on his coffee cups, but before he could get a word out, Cindy was placing a sleeve on his new morning brew and handing it off to him.

"How was your day yesterday, Matthew?" Cindy asked.

Matthew quickly glanced in his rearview mirror to see if any cars were waiting to be served. With a question like that, he had to decide whether he would provide her with an honest answer or a quick one.

"It was a day. Change can be difficult, ya know, and it was a tough day," Matthew said with a smile, hoping to wrap up the conversation.

"The school will become what you *choose* to focus on. You must *BE* the change you want to see. And remember, no duty is more important than giving thanks," Cindy said, still smiling.

How did she always know the right things to say? Matthew wondered. Suddenly another car pulled up behind him, and he had to exit his thoughts so that he could move out of the way for the next customer.

"Today, choose to BE GREAT!" Cindy said as she waved goodbye and prepared to greet her next customer.

Matthew removed the stopper from the hot cup of coffee and tucked it inside the sleeve. He took a small sip and placed the coffee in the cup holder that separated the passenger seat from the driver's seat. Because it was still dark out and he needed to focus on the road, he couldn't see what, if anything, had been written on his cup, but he could hardly wait to find out.

As he pulled into his parking space in front of the school, he sat for several moments imagining all the good things this day could bring. He was still energized from his power hour this morning and couldn't wait to share that energy with his team. He was even excited about his meeting with Ms. Graves. He knew that he would have to begin officially documenting her behavior so that he could start setting boundaries necessary for a safe learning environment.

He thought about Cindy's comments and focused on what he wanted the school to BE. He knew that if the school was going to change, he would have to BE the model for what he wanted to see. Without hesitation he picked up his coffee cup and pulled down the sleeve to reveal his new message. "BE Grateful," the cup read.

Matthew smiled and changed his focus to all the things that brought him joy, even the little things, because he knew that the little things could grow into much bigger things!

15

BElieve

Without hesitation Matthew opened the car door, put on his suit jacket, and threw his backpack across his shoulder. He placed the stopper back into his coffee cup, which was still hot, and headed into the school ready and loaded with positive energy for a new day. No matter what the day would bring, Matthew realized that his greatest strength was how he chose to respond.

As he pulled open the glass door to the front of the school, he was surprised to see bright lights beaming from all directions in every hallway. The floors sparkled and smelled of lemon-scented cleaner, the same wonderful scent he remembered from his time as a teacher.

"Good morning, Mr. Mason!" a voice yelled from the end of one hallway.

It was the head custodian, Mr. Blesin. He had to have been at the school for several hours to accomplish this, Matthew thought.

"Good morning, Mr. Blesin! Good to see you here so early. The floors look and smell amazing!" Matthew said, walking on the tip of his toes to show respect for the shine.

"Thank you, Mr. Mason. I just wanted you to know that you've inspired me to be better," Mr. Blesin said as he slowly approached Matthew armed with an old, dirty mop.

"Well, that makes me happy," Matthew responded. "I know the teachers and students will appreciate what you've done this morning."

"It's been a while since I've felt the energy to clean like this," Mr. Blesin said, looking around at the school with pride. "I think I've been unmotivated ever since they moved me to this school. I always felt it was God's punishment. Now I see it was a blessing in disguise!" Mr. Blesin chuckled as he thought about his comment.

"Where were you before?" Matthew asked curiously.

"I've been with Grace for many years now. I started out at the district office as their head custodian and was then moved to Peace Middle, and I stayed there until they moved me to Mercy. I've been unhappy ever since, until now," Mr. Blesin shared.

"Your energy certainly impacts the energy of others, and the way the building looks and feels this morning gets me excited to start the day," Matthew exclaimed.

"Well, I know you're a busy person, Mr. Mason. I'll let you get to what you were doing. Have a great day!" Mr. Blesin said, walking away to return to his cleaning.

"It's going to be a GREAT day!" Matthew said with a chuckle.

"Indeed it is a great day," Mr. Blesin said, shaking his head as he strolled down the hall.

Matthew looked up to the heavens and said a quick thank-you, acknowledging all the good things that had already happened to him this morning. He opened the door to his office and found that the lights were already on. His carpet had fresh vacuum imprints, his desk and conference table glistened, and on his desk was a brown paper bag with a hand-written message: "Thank you for being here, Mr. Mason.—Mr. Blesin." Inside the bag was a warm kolach. He set his coffee down on his desk and enjoyed a quick bite.

BElieve, Matthew said to himself as he glanced at the BE poster on the wall. It had not even been a full week, but he could see that the power of BElieving in what was possible was making their dreams a reality. He began to see all the challenges as opportunities that would move them closer to realizing their vision.

When he opened his computer, he saw that Ms. Rally had already responded to his email and updated his calendar. His morning was packed with meetings, but he looked forward to them. She had even scheduled some time for a mental health break. These meetings would be the beginning of getting Mercy on a track to success.

Wednesday, January 21

8:30	Meet with Ms. Shields (Ms. Davenport will cover class)
9:15	Talk to bus driver, Bus 165, phone: 455-689-0000
9:45	Meet with Ms. Graves (Ms. Davenport will cover class)
11:00	Lunch with Ms. Helena and Ms. Reeves
11:30	Pause and take a break =)
12:35	Reflection Meeting with Ms. Love

His meeting with Ms. Shields went well. She was just as apologetic in this meeting as she had been in the first one, when they discussed her leaving the faculty meeting. This time, Matthew placed her on a growth plan that challenged her to come up with a process for documenting and tracking students' modes of transportation. She cried and claimed that she had never had a growth plan, but Matthew knew that the safety of her students was too important to ignore.

At 9:15 Matthew called the bus driver, who was adamant that it was not his responsibility to know the stops of students. He argued that he made all the correct stops, and students (even the young ones) needed to know when to get off the bus. The bus driver suggested that Matthew have a teacher ride the bus to make sure students got off at the right stops. Matthew could see that they were not going to come to an agreement, so he called the bus supervisor, who took care of the matter.

Between meetings Matthew called Emma's parents and apologized again for what had happened yesterday. They were still upset about the incident but appreciated him reaching out to inform them of the strategies they were employing to make sure this didn't happen again. He also called to thank Ms. Johnson for bringing Emma to safety.

His meeting with Ms. Graves didn't go well, and he expected that she would blame others and complain that he was out to get her. He was happy that Ms. Reeves could be a part of the discussion and observe as he also placed Ms. Graves on a growth plan to improve her communication/behavior and instructional practices. She threatened to file a grievance against Matthew and claimed he was retaliating against her because she told him the truth. Although they were able to come up with some action items together, he knew that this was not the end of his challenges with Ms. Graves.

Matthew was feeling pretty good about his morning and thought he was making real progress. He hated that he had to place two teachers on a growth plan in his first week, but if things were going to change, he had to first set boundaries. If he continued to allow negative things to happen, they would become a part of the culture.

"Knock, knock." He heard a soft sound at the door. It was Ms. Rally. When Matthew glanced at the clock on his computer, he realized that Ms. Helena would be arriving soon for their meeting.

"Mr. Mason, Mr. Rodriguez is on the line. He wants to know if you're available to talk," Ms. Rally said, poking her head through the door.

"Sure! You can send him through," Matthew announced.

The phone rang a couple of times before Matthew picked up with a cheery voice. "Hello, Mr. Rodriguez, how's it going?"

"It's okay, I guess. I'm calling to see how you're doing," the superintendent said in a grim tone.

Matthew hadn't heard him sound like this since he informed him he would be leaving Grace Schools to take a position with another district. The superintendent rarely sounded down unless something serious was going on.

"I'm great! Just wrapped up a few meetings and getting ready for my next one in a bit, but what's up?" Matthew asked curiously.

"My office received a call from one of your teachers, asking to be transferred because she states you're retaliating against her," the superintendent informed Matthew.

"*Retaliation* is a strong word. May I ask the teacher's name?" Matthew inquired.

"It's Ms. Graves," said Superintendent Rodriguez. "She's been with the district a long time, and she can be a lot of trouble for you," he added.

"I'm fine, Mr. Rodriguez. I've already had two discussions with her, and I placed her on a growth plan this morning to work on a few areas in which I see she needs to improve," said Matthew.

"Well, the reason I'm calling is I'm thinking about moving her to another elementary school, and I just wanted to inform you before I made the switch. I've already had parents calling to advocate for her, accusing you of bullying the teachers. This is not something you need to be dealing with in your first week on the job," the superintendent said in a concerned voice.

"Look, it's not okay that we continue to move her around the district and never address her poor attitude or performance. I would rather she stay here and you allow me to work with her and see if she can improve, rather than put her on someone else. It's not right," Matthew said in a courageous tone.

If things were going to change, they couldn't keep running away or hiding the problem; they would need to address it head-on. Allowing Ms. Graves to get her way would only reinforce her poor behavior.

"If she stays with you, more than likely she's going to file a grievance, and our human resources team will have to conduct an investigation. I don't know if you have time for that with everything else you have on your plate," the superintendent warned.

"I'm not okay with her transferring. Look, I didn't just return to Mercy; I returned to Grace, and if we're going to do what's best for this district, we must be open and honest with people, even if it causes conflict. If you allow her to remain in any role with that attitude, it will become a part of the district culture, and I believe the risks can be great, especially from what I've witnessed from her so far," Matthew said.

"I'll leave it up to you, then, and allow you to handle it," the superintendent said. "Keep in mind she's well connected in the community, and she can make your life a living hell."

"I'm going to do what's right," Matthew reassured him.

"I know you will, and I believe in your leadership, Matthew," the superintendent said before ending the call.

16

BE Awesome!

Matthew was not going to allow Ms. Graves to bully him and push him into a corner. He had returned to Mercy to help save the school and ensure its students received a good education, but so far, his work had nothing to do with the success of students because he was stuck managing the attitudes and behaviors of the adults.

He shook off the call from the superintendent so that he could concentrate on his next meeting. Ms. Helena had a way of bringing in positive energy wherever she went. She didn't have to mumble a word; you could feel it the moment she entered the room.

Shortly after his call with the superintendent, Ms. Helena and Ms. Reeves showed up in his office at the same time.

"Hello, ladies! Come on in," Matthew said, excited to see them and get started. He was happy to talk about something positive for a change.

"How are you today, Mr. Mason?" Ms. Helena said, grinning from ear to ear. Ms. Helena's bun was still neatly in place with a red colored pencil tucked behind her ear. She sported a red top with yellow flowers and green pants. She resembled a botanical garden bursting with colorful blossoms.

"I'm GREAT! How are you ladies?" Matthew asked, remembering his experience with Cindy and her team at the coffee shop that morning.

Just then Ms. Rally entered, along with one of the cafeteria aides holding lunch trays from the cafeteria. "Lunch is served," she said in a cheerful tone. Their trays included cheese pizza, apple sauce, and milk.

"I feel like I'm back in elementary school," Ms. Reeves said as she retrieved her tray and found her seat at the conference table.

"Can I get you anything else?" Ms. Rally asked with her hands clasped in front of her.

"No, this is awesome," Matthew said. "Oh, and thanks for updating my calendar this morning. That was very helpful," he added with a soft smile.

"Oh, I'm just doing my job," said Ms. Rally as she left the room and pulled the door closed behind her.

Matthew, Ms. Reeves, and Ms. Helena took their seats around the conference room table and proceeded to dive into lunch and their discussion.

"Your office is coming together nicely," Ms. Helena said, looking around the room. "I have some artwork that will be perfect for your walls."

"I can't wait to hear about your ideas," Matthew said, anxious to get to the reason for their meeting. "I've been thinking about this meeting since you came to see me yesterday. I'm so happy we could make the time work."

"I'm excited too," said Ms. Helena. "I'm also happy Ms. Reeves could join us." She smiled at Ms. Reeves.

"When you asked us what we wanted Mercy to *BE*, I have to be honest, I didn't see a way forward, until I started thinking about how we could make these things happen," Ms. Helena continued, pointing at the *BE* poster. "After our special-areas team and I talked about it over lunch, we agreed that this is where we want to go. So, if this is where we want to go, what do *we* need to *BE* in order to get there?" Ms. Helena asked enthusiastically.

Matthew couldn't believe what he was hearing. Ms. Helena was confirming everything he had read this morning during his power hour. The mission was the destination, and the team's values (behaviors and attitudes) were how they would get there.

"Please continue," Matthew said, his mouth stuffed with cheese pizza. He was excited to learn more about her idea.

"Let's think about what *we* (the teachers, students, and staff) need to *BE* in order to get Mercy to where it needs to *BE*," Ms. Helena said as she took her first bite of pizza.

"Oh, that's good," Ms. Reeves said, finally speaking up.

"The pizza or the idea?" Matthew joked.

"Definitely the idea," Ms. Reeves chuckled.

"So how do we get started?" Matthew asked, wanting to solicit ideas from the team before sharing his own.

"Well, that's where you two come in," said Ms. Helena. "I manage one classroom on campus, and I know what my students need to be in order to succeed in the art classroom. The two of you have walked this building and know what we *all* need to BE as a school community. I'm sure you've observed enough to understand the attitudes and behaviors we need to embrace to move Mercy out of this dismal state."

"I like what you're saying, Ms. Helena. So let's do this. Let's look at our mission statement. I understand that the district leadership team recently helped each school create a mission statement, right?" Matthew asked.

"Yes, they did," Ms. Helena said, grabbing her cell phone and navigating to Mercy's website.

She read the mission statement aloud: "Our mission is to inspire a community of learners where adults and children feel loved, valued, safe, and encouraged to develop to their fullest potential."

"I love that mission statement!" Matthew exclaimed. "It's short and sweet and packs a punch! I also like that you have included the adults in the mission. A lot of school mission statements only express what they do for students and leave out our teachers and families. This mission is inclusive of everyone as we can all see ourselves in 'a community of learners.'"

Matthew recalled a message from his reading that morning. Jack Welch, author of *Winning*, wrote, "An effective mission statement basically answers one question: How do we intend to win in this business?" Matthew thought for a few moments.

Returning to the conversation, Matthew asked, "How will we know when we've achieved this?" He pushed the two women to think about what winning would look like.

"I think that when *all* of us—that's adults and students—see ourselves as learners who feel loved, valued, safe, and encouraged, we will have achieved this goal," Ms. Reeves said enthusiastically.

"And when we *all* develop to our full potential," added Ms. Helena.

"Exactly! That's winning!" Matthew exclaimed.

Excited, Matthew stood up, grabbed a sheet of chart paper, and secured it to the wall. At the very top, he wrote the words *BE Principles* in big, bold letters. Underneath that he wrote the mission statement.

"So, looking at this mission statement," Matthew said, continuing the discussion, "what are the behaviors that will help us achieve our goals?"

There was silence for a few moments as they all contemplated the mission statement.

"This is where I think you and your cup of coffee come in, Matthew," Ms. Helena chimed in. "In the staff meeting, you introduced the word *BE* that was written on your cup. Since then I'm sure you've envisioned behaviors that will move Mercy forward, right?" she asked with a smile. "I know the other day I saw the message 'BE responsible' written on your cup, and I think that's a good start. If people are going to reach their full potential, they will need to be responsible for their decisions, actions, and results."

"Yes! If teachers and students would take responsibility, that would be a huge win for all of us," Matthew said, adding the first BE Principle to the chart: "Principle 1: BE Responsible."

"Yesterday, when I was in one of the classrooms, I don't think the teacher was aware of how her behavior impacted students' behavior. I also observed this during the assembly, as students were displaying the same behaviors as their teachers. So, I think we need to be aware," Matthew said, adding the second principle: "Principle 2: BE Aware."

There was silence in the room as the three of them stared at the poster. Suddenly Ms. Reeves spoke up. "Matthew, yesterday, during our discussion, I shared with you how my mentors always encouraged me to be open to the possibilities. This means listening to others who may not think as we do or being open to new opportunities," she said with a smile.

Matthew added a third principle: "Principle 3: BE Open."

They stared at their masterpiece, looking back and forth between the mission statement and the *BE* Principles. You could feel the energy from their joint creativity in the room.

"I have had to have some courageous conversations today and take some courageous actions," Matthew shared, thinking about his conversations with the superintendent and Ms. Graves. "Showing courage is often thought of as facing certain situations without fear, but it also involves facing them despite our fears. This is something we all need to embrace if we're going to save Mercy." Matthew wrote the fourth principle on the chart: "Principle 4: BE Courageous."

"Amen! That's a great addition!" Ms. Reeves said, pushing her empty lunch tray to the side to remove any distractions to be totally engaged.

"Did you stop by your coffee shop this morning?" asked Ms. Helena.

"I sure did," said Matthew, holding up his cup.

"Aha! BE Grateful!" Ms. Helena proclaimed looking at the message that adorned Matthew's disposable coffee cup. "We can never underestimate the power of gratitude! You get more of what you focus on; it would be nice to give our attention to the good things that's happening at Mercy!"

Matthew wrote: "Principle 5: BE Grateful."

Ms. Reeves stared at the BE poster the staff had created in the faculty meeting and then at the mission statement again.

"In order to accomplish these things, we must believe we can, right?" she asked. "I know we can't add *BE* to the word *Believe*, but we may be able to come up with another term."

Ms. Helena got up from her seat, took a marker from Matthew's desk, and without saying a word she capitalized the letters B and E in the word believe and added the sixth principle: "Principle 6: BElieve."

"Awesome!" Ms. Reeves shouted.

"Very creative," said Matthew. "Changing our mindset from that of a victim to that of a victor is critical to winning and accomplishing our goals. We must believe that the impossible is possible if we're going to develop to our fullest potential!"

"I think I have the final two values that will complete our list," Matthew said with his marker in hand.

Matthew added the final two principles to the poster:

Principle 7: BE Awesome

Principle 8: BE YOU

The room was silent for a few moments before erupting in cheers, laughter, and high fives!

17

BE YOU!

Eight weeks had passed since the brainstorming session when they had come up with the eight BE Principles. They had invited other team members to join the discussion about what these principles looked like in action and how they could be reinforced throughout the school.

Matthew had invited Ms. Love, the counselor, to discuss ways she could design curriculum to teach these values to all students. She suggested taking things slow to ensure that the students were understanding and applying each principle in school and at home. She decided she would reinforce one principle a month and provide teachers with minilessons to help them teach the values in the classroom.

The music teacher composed a song called "Mercy's Eight BEs," in which the students learned hand motions to go along with the words. They even had the opportunity to perform the song at a district leadership meeting.

Ms. Helena was busy working on posters and banners to be displayed throughout the hallways, cafeteria, restrooms, and classrooms; she even designed one for the bus so that students and teachers were constantly reminded of their eight BEs.

Ms. Reeves was leading a culture committee called The Culture Cre8ors that included voices from teachers, students, and parents. She was excited to have little JJ on the committee, as well as Emma's parents.

Ms. Shields received a grant to start a gardening club, and she was very excited about the opportunity. And as for Ms. Graves, she decided to retire, stating that she just couldn't handle all the talk about the eight BEs.

Everything was going well for Matthew and the Mercy team. Of course, there were the everyday struggles that came with turning around a school, but he always tried to look for the lesson.

This moment in his life reminded him of a message from a book he had read a couple of years ago titled *The Beauty Underneath the Struggle: Creating Your B.U.S. Story*. In it, author Niki Spears writes, "I believe everything happens for a reason. When we can tell ourselves a different story and change the conversations we have with ourselves, we can quickly advance to the next page of our life and resume writing a narrative of which we can be proud."

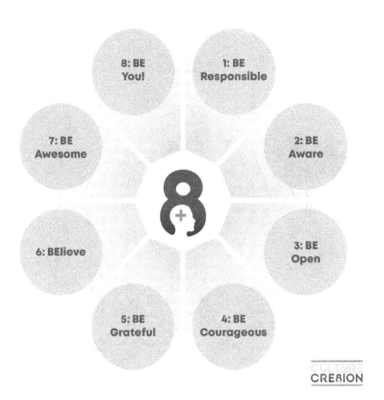

BE *responsible*

"Strength and growth come only through continuous struggle."
—Napoleon Hill

BE *grateful*

"Acknowledging the good you already have in your life is the foundation for all abundance."
—Eckhart Tolle

BElieve

"There is a surrendering to your story and then a knowing that you don't have to stay in your story."
—Collette Baron-Reid

BE *awesome*

"The most creative act you will ever undertake is the act of creating yourself."
—Deepak Chopra